MAKING **GOD** KNOWN

MAKING **GOD** KNOWN

GREG LAURIE

KERYGMA
PUBLISHING

ISBN: 0-9777103-6-x
Published by Allen David Publishers—Dana Point, California
Coordination: FM Management, Ltd.
Editor: Karla Pedrow
Cover design by Chris Laurie
Designed by Highgate Cross + Cathey
Printed in Canada

How then shall they call on Him in whom they have not believed? And how shall they believe in Him of whom they have not heard? And how shall they hear without a preacher? And how shall they preach unless they are sent? As it is written: "How beautiful are the feet of those who preach the gospel of peace, who bring glad tidings of good things!"

Romans 10:14–15

Contents

Introduction: Our Search for Meaning

It has been said there are two things that are true of every person: we all want to be happy, and we are all going to die.

From the moment you and I were born, we have been on a quest. What we have been searching for isn't exactly clear, but we know we want our lives to have some kind of meaning and purpose. We know we want to be happy.

For me, this search began at a very early age. I was born into a chaotic environment. My mother, an alcoholic, married and divorced seven times. I had to grow up fast and learn how to take care of myself. And as I observed the adult world into which I had been immersed, as I watched all the drinking and partying, I thought, *I don't want to live that way.* But by the time I was in high school, I was out drinking and partying with the best of them.

Not only that, but the 1960s drug revolution had emerged on the scene. Rock stars like Jimi Hendrix, Janis Joplin, and Jim Morrison were telling us to expand our minds. I had been told that if I took drugs, I would become more aware. I definitely wanted to be more aware, so I started taking drugs. And I became more aware all right—aware of how miserable I was.

Eventually I went from smoking pot to taking LSD. But as our rock icons died one by one (Jim Morrison, Jimi Hendrix, and Janis Joplin all dead, ironically, at the age of 27), I knew this was not the life I wanted to live.

My search was narrowing through the process of elimination. I knew what I was searching for wasn't in partying. It wasn't in drinking. It wasn't in affluence. It wasn't in drugs. It wasn't in the adult world I had observed.

Then one day on my high school campus, I saw a really cute girl. A friend of mine was talking to her, so I came walking up to them and waited for a chance to introduce myself. As I stood there, I noticed that in addition to a textbook and a notebook, she was carrying an unusual-looking book with a black leather cover and gold pages.

I thought, *Oh, no! That is a Bible. This girl is a Jesus freak. What a waste of a perfectly cute girl!* After all, I thought Christians were all a bit on the crazy side. Something wasn't right about them. Why would anyone come to school carrying a Bible and talking about God as though He were their next-door neighbor? Don't get me wrong—I believed in Jesus. I had seen all His movies, and what I knew about Him (which was not much), I liked. When I was in trouble, I always called on Jesus. He was my God of choice in a crisis. But I never realized that Jesus could be known in a personal way.

So one day at lunchtime, I was walking across the campus and noticed the Christians out on the front lawn, singing songs about God. I sat down a few feet away, close enough where I could eavesdrop on their conversation (because the cute girl was there), but not close enough for my friends to assume that I was actually one of them, which in high school was social suicide. As I listened and watched them sing songs about God, I thought, *Look at these crazy people. ... They are so weird. ... They are so demented. ... And they are so ... happy!* So I tried a new thought on for size: *What if the Christians are right? What if God can be known in a personal way?*

Then a young man named Lonnie, who was a youth pastor, got up and spoke. I don't remember most of what he said, but I do remember one statement that hit me like a lightning bolt. He told the group, "Jesus said, 'You are either for Me or against Me.' " I thought, *Well, these Christians are definitely for Him. And I am not one of them. Does that mean that I am against Him?*

He continued, "If you want to give your life to Jesus right now and be forgiven of your sin, I want you to get up and walk forward, and I am going to lead you in a prayer." *There is no way I could do that,* I thought. *I would like to know God. I would like to have happiness and peace. But this won't work for me. I am not the religious type. I am too cynical, too mad at the world.*

Amazingly, I got up anyway, went forward, and prayed along with a handful kids who had done the same.

It was as though time stood still as I called out to God, "Forgive me of my sin. Come into my life." I remember that as soon as I was done praying, it felt like someone had lifted a big load off my shoulders.

And indeed that was the case. The burden of sin and guilt I had been carrying for the first seventeen years of my life had been removed. Then the school bell rang. Back to class!

But before I left, that really cute girl came up, hugged me, and said, "God bless you, brother." I thought, *This is good being a Christian!* But nothing ever came of that. She and I never became more than just friends. Or as my new Christian friends would say, she was simply "a sister in the Lord."

God used her to get my attention. And as I began to meet other Christians and grow in my newfound faith, I discovered what God was *really* like. I learned what it meant to have a personal relationship with Jesus Christ.

Many people today hold on to preconceived notions about God. Some envision God as an angry, hostile, uptight Supreme Being who is perpetually in a bad mood and just waiting to nail them when they fail or sin. Others may think that God is strange or weird, because they have seen or talked to strange or weird people who call themselves Christians. Yet let's not blame their weirdness on Christianity. They probably were that way in the first place.

So what is God like? How does He look at us? And more importantly, does He approve or disapprove of us? We find the answers in the pages of Scripture, where God reveals himself. And what better expert on the topic than Jesus, who gives us a snapshot of God in the parable of the prodigal son. I think it could be more appropriately called the parable of the loving father, because Jesus portrays God as a heavenly Father who deeply loves us and desperately misses us when we sin or go astray.

It is the story of a boy living at home with his dad and his brother, who one day thought, *I am sick and tired of living here. I am tired of the rules of my father. I am tired of the regulations. I want to go out and live the life that I have chosen to live.* The bright lights of the big city were calling. So he went to his dad and basically said, "Give me the portion of the inheritance that is coming to me. I don't want to wait until you die. I want to experience life now."

So the father gave his son what he asked for, and off the boy went. When he rolled into town, I am sure he was one popular guy ... until the money ran out and his friends with it.

Lacking money and friends, he ended up hanging out with a bunch of pigs. Literally. What began as living high on the hog ended up in hanging out with the hogs. Eventually, even their food was starting to look good.

Suddenly it dawned on him how ridiculous this was. He came to his senses and decided it was time to go back to his father. Suddenly the home that he couldn't get away from fast enough, the home that was so full of rules and regulations, was looking a whole lot better. It dawned on him that everything he wanted in life was there with his dad. He just needed to go home. So he started his journey back.

While he was still a long way off, his father saw him. And not only did he see him, but he started running toward him to embrace him. When this father ran toward his son, he could have stopped short of him and said, "Whoa! Go take a bath, son! (The prodigal had been hanging out with hogs, after all.) Then maybe I will give you a hug." But that isn't what happened. The father accepted him just as he was.

But there is something else to think about. In this culture, it was considered undignified for an older man to run. It just wasn't done. But the father knew that he had to get to his son as quickly as possible. Why? Because this son had drug the family name through the mud. This son had spent his money on wild living and parties and prostitutes. This son had blown it so bad that it was quite possible that people were getting ready to stone him. The father knew that if he could just get to his son and throw his arms around him, his son would be safe. So the father, willing to lose his dignity, pulled his robe above his knees and sprinted toward his son. Then he threw his arms around him and kissed him. The word used for "kissed" in this story could better be translated "smothered him with kisses." The father kissed him over and over and over again. That is how he felt toward his son.

However, he didn't leave his son the way he was. He told his servants, "Bring out the best robe and put it on him, and put a ring on his hand and sandals on his feet. And bring the fatted calf here and kill it, and let us eat and be merry; for this my son was dead and is alive again; he was lost and is found" (Luke 15:22–24).

Like that prodigal, God will accept us as we are. But He doesn't want to leave us that way. He will change us.

That day on my high school campus as I eavesdropped on the Christians' meeting, I knew there was a hole in my heart. I knew there was a God out there somewhere. And when I heard that God could come and live inside me and give me meaning and purpose, when I heard that I could have my guilt removed and go to heaven when I die, it sounded like an offer I could not refuse.

A lot of years have passed since then, yet I have not once regretted my decision to respond to the invitation that was given that day. Jesus Christ has brought meaning and purpose to my life. He has given me a life worth living. And having had the incredible privilege of pointing others to Jesus Christ over the years, I have seen Him do the same for them—time and time again.

The good news of Jesus Christ is as relevant today as it was back then, and these are critical times for sharing it. There are doors that are open today that may not necessarily stay open forever. Speaking to the last days church, Jesus said, "See, I have set before you an open door, and no one can shut it … " (Revelation 3:8). And speaking to His disciples, He said, "Behold, I say to you, lift up your eyes and look at the fields, for they are already white for harvest!" (John 4:35).

You might be thinking, *Amen! I pray that the Lord will raise up more people to go out and share the Good News.* But no one can honestly pray that this work will be done who is not actually willing to help do it. We all have a part to play. Granted, not all of us are full-time pastors, evangelists, or missionaries, but all of us are called to sow seeds. Everyone has a part to play. That means you. That means me. Unbelievers are not the enemy—they are people for whom Christ died. We need to remember it wasn't that long ago that we were among them.

Are you a laborer in the harvest? The complainers are many. The observers are many. The spectators are many. The critics are many. But the laborers are few. We need laborers in the harvest. Will you become one?

Greg Laurie
March 2007
Riverside, California

1 First-Century Principles for Reaching the Twenty-first Century

Does the idea of speaking to a total stranger about Christ cause you to get very nervous? Have you ever tried to tell someone about Jesus and had it go nowhere? Have you ever had a difficult question asked about your faith that you did not have the answer to? Then this book is for you!

As I will point out later, we way overcomplicate this thing we call evangelism. It is my firm belief that God can use you to bring others into His kingdom. Otherwise, why would God have commanded us to do so? The calling of God is the enabling of God, and I believe that He wants to use all believers to bring people to himself. We are told in Proverbs 11:30, "The fruit of the righteous is a tree of life, and he who wins souls is wise." And Daniel 12:3 says, "Those who are wise shall shine like the brightness of the firmament, and those who turn many to righteousness like the stars forever and ever." God wants you to turn others to righteousness. God wants you to win souls.

We must take hold of the moment or we may lose it forever.

According to one poll, nine out of ten American adults cannot accurately define the meaning of the Great Commission. Seven in ten adults have no clue what "John 3:16" means. And barely one-third know the meaning of the expression, "the gospel." We may be thinking, *They aren't believers, so what do you expect?* But the most alarming statistic of all is that 95 percent of Christians have never led another person to Christ.

This book can help with all that and more. God wants to use you to bring others to himself. That's a fact. Let's find out how together.

Billy Graham has said,

> The evangelistic harvest is always urgent. The destiny of men and of nations is always being decided. Every generation is crucial; every generation is strategic. ... God will hold us responsible at the Judgment Seat of Christ for how well we fulfilled our responsibilities and took advantage of our opportunities."[1]

I believe the world today is actually hungry for the message we have to offer. It seems to me that people are in a spiritual search mode—especially young people. There are opportunities for sharing this message that will be either seized or lost. We must take hold of the moment or we may lose it forever.

I'm well aware that we live in a postmodern world where moral relativism is the rule of the day. Some may feel as though the time to present absolute truth has passed. We can only ask questions, but not offer answers, they would say. But, to borrow a word from the British, that's *rubbish*. Regardless of the trends of contemporary culture, truth is still truth. In spite of our dramatic advances in technology, the essential needs of humanity remain the same, as does the answer to their problems.

We are called to bring the gospel to our generation, but many of us are not doing that. It seems to me that many Christians are out of touch with our culture today. Some of us seem to have forgotten that we are living in the twenty-first century.

It reminds me of the woman who accompanied her husband to his doctor's appointment. Afterward, the doctor called her into his office and said, "Your husband is suffering from a very severe disease, combined with horrible stress. If you don't do the following, your husband will surely die.

"Each morning, fix him a healthy breakfast. Be pleasant, and make sure he is in a good mood. For lunch, make him a nutritious meal. For dinner, prepare an especially nice meal for him. Don't burden him with chores, as he probably will have had a hard day.

Don't discuss your problems with him; it only will make his stress worse. And, most importantly, smother your husband with affection and kiss him constantly. Make every effort to satisfy his every whim.

"If you can do this for the next ten to twelve months, then I think your husband will regain his health completely."

On the way home, the husband asked his wife, "So, what did the doctor say?"

It seems to me that many Christians
are out of touch with our culture today.

"You're going to die," she replied.

Like this woman, some Christians would rather disregard a lost soul than change their methods. We live in a sin-sick world, and we need to do everything we can to reach people. As God told the prophet Isaiah, "So shall My word be that goes forth from My mouth; it shall not return to Me void, but it shall accomplish what I please, and it shall prosper in the thing for which I sent it" (Isa. 55:11).

Paul's Playbook

I believe that the principles used in the first century for proclaiming the gospel still hold true for us today. In Acts 17, we find a page right out of the apostle Paul's playbook as we observe this master communicator bringing his message to Athens. At that time, Athens was the cultural and intellectual center of the world. Athens was heir to the great philosophers Socrates, Plato, Aristotle, and others who established patterns of thought that have affected human learning for centuries. Almost all philosophies follow, to some degree, the teachings of these men.

While Paul was in Athens, he did what any Athens tourist would do. He went sightseeing. There were magnificent architectural edifices, statues, and images erected to every deity imaginable.

You name it, and the Athenians had erected some kind of representation to a god they thought existed. But he was grieved to see the absolute absence of the living God. Instead, there was every imaginable substitute.

Have you ever felt that way as you look at our confused society? Do you ever find yourself channel surfing, and as you look at all of the things that are being offered to our culture today, you find yourself getting angry? We have a choice: We can wring our hands in exasperation and complain about the state of affairs in our world. Or, we can do something about it: take the gospel to the world. Paul could have cursed the darkness, but instead he turned on the light. And that brings us to our first principle of effective evangelism.

Does your heart ache for lost people?

Principle 1:
Effective evangelism always begins with a burden.

Effective evangelism always begins with a burden. Paul's message began when his spirit was stirred. He was grieved to see the absolute absence of the living God and, in His place, every conceivable substitute. So he took action. Acts 17 tells us,

> While Paul was waiting for them in Athens, he was greatly distressed to see that the city was full of idols. So he reasoned in the synagogue with the Jews and the God-fearing Greeks, as well as in the marketplace day by day with those who happened to be there. (vv. 16–17 NIV)

The phrase "greatly distressed" in verse 16 could be literally translated, "exasperated" or "irritated and roused to anger." In other words, Paul was hot and mad.

Moved to Action
One of the reasons we don't effectively reach our culture is because we are woefully out of touch, living in our own Christian subculture.

And to be honest, many of us don't really care about people who do not know the Lord. This is hard for some of us to admit. If some of us were to be brutally honest, we would have to say that we don't have that burden. Paul was burdened to the point that he declared, "Woe is me if I do not preach the gospel!" (1 Cor. 9:16). We simply have to care, or nothing will happen in the way of effective evangelism. Does your heart ache for lost people?

C. H. Spurgeon knew the need for such a burden when he said, "The Holy Spirit will move them by first moving you. If you can rest without their being saved, they will rest too. But if you are filled with an agony for them, if you cannot bear that they should be lost, you will soon find that they are uneasy too."[2]

Principle 2:
Effective evangelists need to know their audience.

We need to know the people we are speaking to. Paul went right to where these people were and brought the gospel to them. It is important for us to have contact with—to be out and among—the people we are speaking to. Jesus certainly modeled this. Time and time again, we see Him breaking free from the multitudes to bring the message to one individual. From the midst of a crowd, He called Zacchaeus out of the tree. … In the blazing noonday sun, He engaged the Samaritan woman in conversation. … And He managed a late-night meeting with the religious man, Nicodemus. Jesus always had time for people, and we should too, be it day or night.

Build a Bridge

That is why one of the best ways to share the gospel is to listen and ask questions, because I have discovered that everyone's favorite subject is themselves. You can turn a monologue into a dialogue by saying, "Tell me about yourself," or asking, "What do you think about this or that?" As you do so, you are learning about and better understanding that person. And because you have taken the time to listen to what they have to say, it's more likely they will be willing to listen to you.

We see Paul taking the time to familiarize himself with these people and what they believed. He examined their idols. He read their poets. He understood their culture. And He wanted to build a bridge to them:

> Therefore he reasoned in the synagogue with the Jews and with the Gentile worshipers, and in the marketplace daily with those who happened to be there. Then certain Epicurean and Stoic philosophers encountered him. And some said, "What does this babbler want to say?" Others said, "He seems to be a proclaimer of foreign gods," because he preached to them Jesus and the resurrection. (vv. 17–18)

Jesus always had time for people, and we should too.

The Epicureans and the Stoics

There were two primary groups that Paul was addressing in Athens: the Epicureans and the Stoics, representing the two dominant schools of thought at this time.

According to the Epicureans' founder, Epicurus, the chief goal of life was to attain the maximum amount of pleasure and the minimum amount of pain. The Epicureans believed the world came about by chance, a random concourse of atoms, and that there would be no afterlife or future judgment. Their basic belief was that this life is all there is. You only go around once, so if it feels good, do it. If it doesn't feel good, don't do it. Avoid what hurts or causes pain. You could say they were the party animals of the first century.

The Epicurean mentality is still with us today, as this way of thinking is so common in our culture. The Bible even points out that this mindset will be prevalent in the last days: "But know this, that in the last days perilous times will come: For men will be lovers of themselves, lovers of money, … without self-control, … haughty, *lovers of pleasure rather than lovers of God"* (2 Tim. 3:1–3, emphasis mine). The Bible also warns against embracing this philosophy: "She who lives in pleasure is dead while she lives" (1 Tim. 5:6).

In contrast to the Epicureans, the Stoics were more disciplined, shunning the pursuit of pleasure. Founded by a man name Zeno, the Stoic philosophy taught self-mastery. The Stoics' goal in life was to reach a place of indifference to pleasure or pain. Zeno taught that life is filled with good and bad. Because you cannot avoid the bad, you must try to grin and bear it. The Stoics believed that God was in everything material: in the spirit of the trees, plants, animals, mountains, and fields. The Stoics' descendants are among us today as well. These are people who have no sense of God or His will for their lives. They just do the best they can, and if bad comes, they just try to be strong and endure it.

Yet both of these philosophies are wrong in that they both reject God. After all, if you don't know God, then you will put something else in His place.

Principle 3:
Effective evangelism must be culturally relevent.

Paul could have blasted his listeners with both barrels. But amazingly, he sought instead to build a bridge to them and quoted one of their own poets: "For in Him we live and move and have our being, as also some of your own poets have said, 'For we are also His offspring' " (v.28).

> If you don't know God, then you will put something else in His place.

It is so important that our listeners know we are living in the same world as they are. We don't necessarily want to build our message on these issues, but to completely ignore them is to miss an opportunity. We need to keep up with the times. Far too often, those of us who are called to communicate are out of touch with the people we are speaking to. The Bible speaks of the leaders of the tribe of Issachar, "who had understanding of the times, to know what Israel ought to do" (1 Chron. 12:32).

The Downside of a Christian Subculture

We can immerse ourselves in our Christian subculture with our own language that no one else can understand: "Are you washed in the blood, sanctified, and a part of the body?" and "Just make sure you are not living in the flesh!" Meanwhile, the person listening is thinking, *Let's see, I need to be part of the body, but not live in the flesh. . . .* I am not suggesting that we stop using biblical terms; we just need to define them. Far too often, we are answering questions that no one is asking and failing to answer the ones that are being asked.

It is so important that our listeners
know we are living in the same world.

Jesus made an interesting statement on this subject: "For the sons of this world are more shrewd in their generation than the sons of light" (Luke 16:8). The "sons of this world" are far more shrewd in the way they present their message and advertise their wares. Meanwhile, it is all too common in the Christian community to put out mediocre presentations. The problem is that the devil never goes on vacation. He never goes to sleep. He is ever vigilant to pull more and more people into his web of destruction.

The objective of effective communication
is to build a bridge, not burn one.

A number of years ago, I was invited to address the members of the National Religious Broadcasters at their annual convention. I asked why we settle for mediocrity and low standards in the Christian media. We are no longer living in the 1950s; it is the twenty-first century. Why can't our graphics be cutting-edge? Why can't our music be fresh and original—not rehashed copies of something else? Why can't our TV and radio productions be attuned to the culture we are speaking to? Why can't our movies be well-crafted, done with artistic integrity without shrouding the message? I believe that they can.

At the time of this writing, some dramatic advances have been made in Christian music and movies with a faith message.

I am not arguing for sensationalism, although I would prefer that to stagnation. I will not compromise our message one iota. But Jesus did say that the sons of this world are more shrewd in their generation than we are. So I say beat them at their own game. Be culturally relevant and speak their language, but deliver the message they need to hear.

The problem lies in the often odd, out-of-touch, even bizarre way we present our message. I would venture to say there are some Christians today who are not persecuted for righteousness' sake—they are persecuted for being just plain weird!

Keep It Interesting

Paul's message aroused the interest of his listeners. The first thing he did was to build a bridge to his audience:

> Then Paul stood in the midst of the Areopagus and said, "Men of Athens, I perceive that in all things you are very religious; for as I was passing through and considering the objects of your worship, I even found an altar with this inscription: TO THE UNKNOWN GOD. Therefore, the One whom you worship without knowing, Him I proclaim to you." (vv. 22–23)

The One whom you worship without knowing, Him I proclaim to you. … Now that was a diplomatic way for Paul to begin his message. He could have said, "You are a bunch of pagans, and you're going to burn!" Technically, that would have been true. But the objective of effective communication is to build a bridge, not burn one. So Paul sought to find something in common with these so-called religious people. Along the same lines, Paul said,

> Even though I am a free man with no master, I have become a slave to all people to bring many to Christ. … Yes, I try to find common ground with everyone, doing everything I can to save some. I do everything to spread the Good News and share in its blessings. (1 Cor. 9:19, 22–23 NLT)

Far too often, unbelievers only know Christians for what we are against instead of knowing what we are for. They know we are against abortion, sexual immorality, and same-sex marriage. But do they know that we are for Jesus? Jesus was strongly criticized for eating and drinking with sinners. But He was doing this to reach them rather than repel them.

The classic example is Jesus in His encounter with the Samaritan woman, whom I mentioned earlier. He could have said, "You are an immoral woman, and you're going to hell!" That would have been essentially true. But instead He sought to establish a dialogue with her. The Bible says that it is the goodness of God that leads us to repentance (see Romans 2:4). Jesus appealed to the emptiness that drove her to her immorality, and He ended up with a real convert that day.

Allow me to share a few thoughts with those of you who might be in ministry or engaged in some kind of public speaking where you share the gospel message with others. Some certainly seem to do a better job at this than others.

There is no excuse for not communicating the gospel well.

I am amazed at how someone can take the life-changing, action-packed Word of God and actually make it boring. I cannot think of a torment worse for me than listening to bad preaching. I heard a story of a minister who was asked to say a few words at a luncheon. He had been instructed to speak for about five minutes, but soon he had gone to ten minutes and then fifteen minutes. The moderator was clearing his throat, hoping the good reverend would notice it was time to stop. The preacher continued to speak. So the moderator actually pounded down his gavel. But on the minister droned. Twenty minutes had gone by, and people were getting upset. A few walked out. Finally, the moderator continuously pounded his gavel for the preacher to cease and desist. Still, the minister would not stop speaking.

In frustration, the moderator threw his gavel at the preacher, narrowly missing him, and instead hitting an elderly man who had fallen asleep in the front row. The man woke up, heard the preacher still speaking, and mumbled to the moderator, "Hit me again! I can still hear him!"

> ## Even the great apostle Paul had days when the response was minimal.

There is no excuse for not communicating the gospel well. Paul said, "For I am not ashamed of the gospel of Christ, for it is the power of God to salvation … " (Rom. 1:16). There is explosive power in the message of the gospel. We don't need to add to it or take away from it. We don't need to complicate it or gloss it over. We just need to proclaim it and let God do His work.

Principle 4:
Effective evangelism must be biblical.

Paul's message was biblical. He opened with a cultural connection, but then took his listeners to the Word of God. This is important because, as I wrote earlier, God's Word will never return void (see Isa. 55:11). I have heard so many evangelists begin with a humorous illustration or a tear-jerking story, and then essentially build their entire message on it. They will read a biblical text, which is nothing more than a point of departure, and then go back to their endless stories and jokes. This is a grave error. Never build a message on an illustration. Always build it on the Word of God. God did not say that clever illustrations would not return void; He said that His Word would not return void.

The great preacher C. H. Spurgeon said, "A sermon is the house; illustrations are the windows that let light in." Don't build a house of glass, yet don't build a house without any windows, either. I have seen that glazed look coming over people's faces while I am explaining a term like justification, only to see them spring back when a simple illustration is used.

Certainly Jesus modeled this for us in His use of parables, which are earthly stories with a heavenly meaning—illustrations, in other words. Matthew 13:34 tells us, "Jesus always used stories and illustrations like these when speaking to the crowds. In fact, he never spoke to them without using such parables" (NLT).

Where the Power Is

Illustrations certainly have their place, but the power is in God's Word. Paul reminded Timothy of the power and sufficiency of Scripture:

> From childhood you have known the Holy Scriptures, which are able to make you wise for salvation through faith which is in Christ Jesus. All Scripture is given by inspiration of God, and is *profitable* for doctrine, for reproof, for correction, for instruction in righteousness, that the man of God may be complete, thoroughly equipped for every good work.
> (2 Tim. 3:15–17, emphasis mine)

The word "profitable" in verse 16 above focuses on the fact that Scripture is sufficient. Everything we need to know about God is found in the Bible. We don't need some "new" revelation. As it's been said, if it is new, it's not true; if it is true, it's not new. The objective is not to make the Bible relevant, because it *is* relevant. However, if we do not believe, as Paul stated, that "all Scripture is given by inspiration of God," then we will have problems from the very beginning.

Principle 5:
Effective evangelism must focus on Jesus, crucified and risen.

An effective evangelistic message will always make a beeline to the cross. Paul concluded his message in Athens with, "He has appointed a day on which He will judge the world in righteousness by the Man whom He has ordained. He has given assurance of this to all by raising Him from the dead" (v. 31). I have been amazed to hear entire evangelistic messages that make only a passing reference to the cross at best.

I once asked Billy Graham, "After all these years of preaching, if you knew as a younger preacher what you know now, what would you emphasize more?" Without a missing a beat, he said, "I would preach more on the cross of Christ and on the blood. That is where the power is." How important that is. And when we fail to do this, we effectively water down the message of the gospel.

> Remorse is being sorry, while repentance is being sorry enough to stop.

Paul warned against this, pointing out that God had called him "to preach the gospel, not with wisdom of words, lest the cross of Christ should be made of no effect. For the message of the cross is foolishness to those who are perishing, but to us who are being saved it is the power of God" (1 Cor. 1:17–18). The phrase "of no effect" could be literally translated, "deprived of its power."

Paul also said that he "determined not to know anything ... except Jesus Christ and Him crucified" (1 Cor. 2:2). Paul recognized there is distinct power in the simple message of the life, words, death, and resurrection of Jesus Christ from the dead. This cannot be emphasized enough.

Principle 6:
Effective evangelism presents the whole gospel.

Paul used a word that we rarely hear these days: *repent.* He told his audience in Athens,

> Truly, these times of ignorance God overlooked, but now commands all men everywhere to repent, because He has appointed a day on which He will judge the world in righteousness by the Man whom He has ordained. He has given assurance of this to all by raising Him from the dead. (vv. 30–31)

This was a command from God himself. Paul didn't say, "I'd suggest you repent," or "I'd advise you to repent," or even "I hope you repent." He said that God "commands all men everywhere to repent."

Then he went on to give three reasons as to why they should repent:

1. There is a day of judgment coming (v. 30). God has appointed a day in which He will judge the world.

2. There is an unchallengeable Judge (v. 31). The one who will do the evaluating will be God.

3. There is an irrefutable fact (v. 31). God has made this evident by an irrefutable fact, which is that He raised this Man (Jesus) from the dead.

> Paul used a word that we rarely hear these days: *repent*.

The Entire Gospel

Rarely do we hear about judgment in our day and age. Yet if we fail to talk about it, then we are not declaring the whole counsel of God. I am not suggesting that we preach "hellfire and brimstone," but we do want to help people fully appreciate the good news of Jesus Christ. And to do that, they must first understand the bad news of their situation. If we don't tell people they need to repent, then we have not told them the entire gospel.

There are a lot of people who feel remorse for their sin, but they never truly repent. Remorse is being sorry, while repentance is being sorry enough to stop. "Godly sorrow brings repentance that leads to salvation and leaves no regret, but worldly sorrow brings death" (2 Cor. 7:10 NIV).

There is such a thing as phony repentance. Phony repentance is like crying when you chop an onion: the eye sheds tears because it is irritated—not because the heart is broken. Repentance means a change of mind and a confession of wrongdoing. It means to turn around, to change one's direction, and to change both the mind and will. Repentance does not denote just any change, but is always a change from wrong to right, away from sin to righteousness.

When Paul stood before the Roman Governor Agrippa, he told of how, on the road to Damascus, Jesus met him and told him,

> "I will deliver you from the Jewish people, as well as from the Gentiles, to whom I now send you, *to open their eyes*, in order *to turn them from darkness to light*, and *from the power of Satan to God*, that they may *receive forgiveness of sins and an inheritance* among those who are sanctified by faith in Me."
> (Acts 26:17–18, emphasis mine)

Paul laid out for Agrippa (and for us today) the process of salvation, which clearly includes repentance:

1. We must have our spiritual eyes opened.
2. We must turn from darkness to light and from the power of Satan to God.
3. We will receive, as a result, the forgiveness of sins and an inheritance.

Paul told his listeners there was a coming judgment. And he told them they needed to repent. Yet this is left out of a lot of preaching today. Our job is not just to make people feel good. It is to tell them the truth.

Principle 7:
Effective evangelism leaves
the results in the hands of God.

God will hold us responsible for proclaiming the truth and being faithful. But the rest is up to Him. Even the great apostle Paul had days when the response was minimal. I take a measure of comfort from the fact that one of the greatest communicators of all time didn't have the most successful meeting imaginable:

> And when they heard of the resurrection of the dead, some mocked, while others said, "We will hear you again on this matter." So Paul departed from among them. However, some men joined him and believed, among them Dionysius the Areopagite, a woman named Damaris, and others with them. (vv. 32–34)

Reactions to the Gospel

The word "mocked" in verse 32 could be translated "some of them sneered and burst out laughing." Paul had just shared the gospel, and they started laughing in his face. These elitists, who thought they were so brilliant, dismissed out of hand the preaching of the gospel from one of the greatest preachers in the history of the church.

Conversion is the work of God and God alone.

This is a reminder to us that no matter how effectively you communicate, some people will react that way. And it will hurt. But that is just the way it is. It happened to Paul; it will happen to you. That is why you need to be praying that God will open their eyes and help them see the reality of what you are saying.

While some mocked, others delayed. They succumbed to the curse of intellectual, academic detachment—the delay tactic: "We will hear you again on this matter" (v. 32). Many intellectuals today use the same tactic: "You know, those are interesting points you have brought up. I will think about this."

Even though some mocked and some delayed, there were some who believed: "However, some men joined him and believed, among them Dionysius the Areopagite, a woman named Damaris, and others with them" (v. 34). Dionysius the Areopagite was one of the judges, an intellectual and a ruler of the city. Along with him was a woman named Damaris and some others.

D. L. Moody said, "I would a great deal rather see a hundred men thoroughly converted, truly born of God, than to see a thousand professed conversions where the Spirit of God has not convicted of sin." I would rather have fewer people who have a real understanding of what the gospel is respond to its message than to have a multitude respond who didn't have a clue.

Conversion is the work of God and God alone. Yes, He uses us, but we must be completely dependent on Him for the results. Many of our attempts at sharing the gospel fail because we do so in our own strength. We are like the disciples who fished all night and caught nothing, only to see everything change when Jesus came on board.

It is actually a great relief for me to know that my responsibility is to lovingly, accurately, and clearly proclaim the gospel. The actual work of conversion is God's part. Jesus said, "No one can come to Me unless the Father who sent Me draws him; and I will raise him up at the last day" (John 6:44).

We need to remember that it is all in the hands of God. At the same time, we are foolish if we congratulate ourselves for great successes. We are also fools if we condemn ourselves for times when our message doesn't resonate. It is the gospel. The results are up to Him. All that God holds me responsible for is faithfulness and proclamation, not how many people were in attendance or even how many people responded. That is not my job. People don't convert people—the Holy Spirit does.

Our job, if you will, is to proclaim the gospel faithfully, lovingly, accurately, clearly, and understandably, and then let the Lord do His work with His message in His way.

The Seven Principles of Effective Evangelism

Principle 1   Effective evangelism always begins with a burden.

Principle 2   Effective evangelists need to know their audience.

Principle 3   Effective evangelism must be culturally relevent.

Principle 4   Effective evangelism must be biblical.

Principle 5   Effective evangelism must focus on Jesus, crucified and risen.

Principle 6   Effective evangelism presents the whole gospel.

Principle 7   Effective evangelism leaves the results in the hands of God.

2 The Three W's of Evangelism

The first time I had ever attempted to share my faith, I was 17 years old and had been a Christian for about two weeks. I had heard that I was supposed to go out tell others about Jesus. So I thought, *Well, I have been a believer now for two entire weeks. I know quite a bit.* It seemed like I knew a lot at the time—a lot more than I used to know, at least. But I knew I wanted to share what God had done for me, because my life had changed so dramatically in such a short period of time.

> We way overcomplicate this
> thing we call evangelism.

So I went out on the beach, armed with my Bible and a copy of a little yellow booklet from Campus Crusade for Christ called *The Four Spiritual Laws.* This material was so new to me that I hadn't even memorized the contents of the booklet yet. As I walked along, looking for someone who wouldn't give me too hard of a time, I saw a woman who looked about the same age as my mother. I thought she probably would be pretty friendly. As I walked up to her, I was so nervous. My mouth was dry. With voice shaking, I said, "Hi. How are you today?"

She looked at me. "Fine, young man. How are you?"

"Oh, I am really good. Yeah. You know, I—I just—uh, you know, I wanted to read something to you. Could I do that?"

"Sure."

So I sat down and started to read that little yellow booklet verbatim. As I said, I hadn't even memorized the contents of it yet. "*The Four Spiritual Laws.* ... Law one: God loves you and has a wonderful plan for your life. ..." And I kept reading, page after page.

Meanwhile, I was thinking to myself, *What on earth am I doing? There is no way she'll become a Christian. This is a complete waste of time.* But then I thought, *I'm already committed. I have to finish.* So I just kept reading. I read the last sentence: "Is there any good reason why you should not accept Jesus Christ right now?" Realizing that was a question, I looked up at her.

She said, "No."

"OK . . . no." I looked back down. Then it dawned on me. I looked up again. "Does that mean yes—you want to accept Christ right now?"

She said, "Yes, I do."

"Well, let's just bow our heads for a word of prayer," I said in the most reverent tone I could muster. (I had heard the pastor at church do that.)

As she closed her eyes, I was frantically searching the booklet for what to do next. The problem was that I had planned for failure and not success. Eventually I found a prayer, which she repeated after me. Meanwhile, I was thinking, *This isn't going to work. This isn't real. This can't be happening.* But it was.

When we were done praying, she opened her eyes and said, "Something just happened to me."

> ## For many of us, it is the Great Omission instead of the Great Commission.

Something had just happened to me too. I got a taste of what it was like to be used by God! I was so young in the faith that I didn't know any better. I wasn't aware that in most circles, the approach I had just used (successfully, I might add) would have fallen far short as a model for personal evangelism. Though I had very little information, I did have a burden for lost people. A lot of it had to do with what God had done for me, because as Jesus said, "For everyone to whom much is given, from him much will be required; and to whom much has been committed, of him they will ask the more" (Luke 12:48). I was as lost as a person could be, but God graciously called me to himself and forgave me.

There is something to be said for the excitement of youth. It's probably why kids are so tech-savvy and can fix their parents' computers. Adults are afraid to try. But kids just jump right in and start pushing buttons.

The primary way God has chosen to reach people is through people.

I am not suggesting that we neglect preparing ourselves to share the gospel. But I am suggesting that we way overcomplicate this thing we call evangelism. In this chapter, I want to look at the three W's of evangelism—the *who, where,* and *why* of evangelism. Let's start with *who.*

The First W: Who?

Who is called to go into all the world and preach the gospel? Answer: *We are.* Matthew 28:19–20, known as the Great Commission, tells us,

> "Go therefore and make disciples of all the nations, baptizing them in the name of the Father and of the Son and of the Holy Spirit, teaching them to observe all things that I have commanded you; and lo, I am with you always, even to the end of the age."

In the original language, the implication is that these words are addressed to everyone—not only pastors, evangelists, and missionaries, but everyone, from businessmen to homemakers to students. No one is exempt.

Also in the original language, these words are *a command.* Jesus was not saying, "If you can find time in your busy schedules, as a personal favor to Me, would you mind at least making an attempt to go into all the world and preach the gospel?" Instead, He was saying, "As your Commander in Chief, as your Lord, as your Master who purchased you with His own blood, I am commanding you—I am ordering you—to go into the world and preach the gospel."

Many of us give up so easily.

The Bible says that we have been redeemed by Christ. The word "redeem" is an interesting word that means "to be bought out of a slave market." Imagine being a slave in shackles, about to be sold, when Jesus arrives and purchases you. Then He tells you that you are free. Wouldn't you want to serve, for the rest of your life, the One who would do that for you? As Paul reminds us, "Or do you not know that your body is the temple of the Holy Spirit who is in you, whom you have from God, and you are not your own? For you were bought at a price; therefore glorify God in your body and in your spirit, which are God's" (1 Cor. 6:19–20).

As we recognize all that God has done for us, it should be our delight, our joy, and indeed our privilege to obey His command and go into all the world and preach the gospel. These words are given to every disciple of Jesus. We should all be saying, "Lord, what is it that You want me to do? I want to fulfill Your command."

Chosen to Produce Fruit

Jesus said, "This is to my Father's glory, that you bear much fruit, showing yourselves to be my disciples. ... You did not choose me, but I chose you and appointed you to go and bear fruit—fruit that will last" (John 15:8, 16 NIV). He chose you and me, before we were even born, to glorify Him and bear fruit. Everything else is secondary. So what is the fruit that Jesus has called us to bear?

Living a godly and holy life is bearing fruit. As Paul reminds us, "But now having been set free from sin, and having become slaves of God, you have your fruit to holiness, and the end, everlasting life" (Rom. 6:22).

Winning others to Jesus Christ and helping them to grow spiritually is fruit. Again, writing to his friends at Rome, Paul said, "I want you to know, dear brothers and sisters, that I planned many times to visit you, but I was prevented until now. I want to work among you and see *spiritual fruit,* just as I have seen among other Gentiles" (Rom. 1:15, emphasis mine). And Proverbs says, "The fruit of the righteous is a tree of life, and he who wins souls is wise" (11:30).

The Great Commission of Matthew 28:19–20 has never been called the Great Suggestion. It was never a suggestion of Jesus that we, His redeemed servants, make disciples of all nations. It was—and is—His command. If I am His disciple, then I am commanded to go and make disciples of others. If I am not making disciples of others, then I am not really being the disciple He wants me to be. But for many of us, it is the Great Omission instead of the Great Commission. We are simply not fulfilling it. And to not do what God has called us to do is a sin, as James 4:17 tells us: "Anyone, then, who knows the good he ought to do and doesn't do it, sins" (NIV).

It is not always easy for me to share the gospel.

While it may be true that not every believer has been gifted as an evangelist, it is also true that every believer still has been called to evangelism. The idea of evangelism seems daunting, overwhelming. How can we do it? As it's been said, the way to eat an elephant is one bite at a time. And the way to fulfill the Great Commission is one person at a time. This brings us to the second "W" of evangelism

The Second W: Where?

Where are we to preach the gospel? Answer: *Everywhere.* In Mark, we are given a variation of the Great Commission: "And He said to them, 'Go into all the world and preach the gospel to every creature'" (Mark 16:15). Former Speaker of the House, Tip O'Neill, once said, "All politics is local," and I believe the same could be said of world evangelism. Go into all *your* world and preach the gospel—into your family, into your workplace, into your campus, into your sphere of influence.

Jesus began the Great Commission with "Go *therefore* and make disciples of all the nations ... " (Matt. 28:19, emphasis mine). What was the "therefore" He was speaking of? We find the answer in the previous verse: "And Jesus came and spoke to them, saying, 'All authority has been given to Me in heaven and on earth'" (v. 18). If the authority is in Him, and He is living inside us, His followers, then His power and resources are at our disposal to accomplish this task.

What Making Disciples Means

So what then, is this task of making disciples? Matthew 28:20 defines it as "teaching them to observe all things that I have commanded you." Simply put, it means to teach them to observe what He has commanded. It is to live our faith in this world and to also share it with others. It is to teach it by word and model it by example. So the full concept of going into all the world and making disciples is to share our faith, to seek to lead people to Christ, and then, to the best of our ability, help them mature spiritually. Colossians 1:28 sums it up well: "We proclaim him, admonishing and teaching everyone with all wisdom, so that we may present everyone perfect in Christ" (NIV).

Now let's look at the third W of evangelism.

> These are critical, strategic
> times for sharing the gospel.

The Third W: Why?

Why are we to do this? Answer: *God has chosen to reach people through people.* Why doesn't God simply poke His face out of the heavens and say, "Believe in Me!"? Why does He want to use flawed people like us? I don't really know the answer to those questions, but I know that He does. As Romans 10:14–15 reminds us,

> How then shall they call on Him in whom they have not
> believed? And how shall they believe in Him of whom they
> have not heard? And how shall they hear without a preacher?
> And how shall they preach unless they are sent? As it is written:
> "How beautiful are the feet of those who preach the gospel
> of peace, who bring glad tidings of good things!"

The primary way God has chosen to reach people is through people—people like you and me.

What about "Lifestyle" Evangelism?

The primary way we are to share this message is verbally. That is not to say that you should not live it first, for indeed you should. But the Bible does not advocate what some call "lifestyle evangelism," meaning that you just live a Christian life and wait for someone to ask you about it. It is a wonderful compliment when that happens, of course, and we should all live in such a way that people will want to know what makes us tick. But at the same time, we need to initiate and verbalize our faith.

In Acts 8, we find the story of a powerful, wealthy dignitary from Ethiopia who had gone to Jerusalem searching for God. Instead of finding the vibrant faith of the glory days of David and Solomon, he found a cold, dead ritualistic faith that offered him little. But he happened to obtain a scroll containing Isaiah 53. As he was reading the words, "He was led as a lamb to the slaughter, and as a sheep before its shearers is silent, … " Philip approached him on the road from Jerusalem to Gaza and asked if he understood what he was reading. The dignitary replied, "How can I, unless someone guides me?" (Acts 8:31). That is what people need and what many want: someone to show them the way—someone like you.

You might find this surprising, but it is not always easy for me to share the gospel. When I am behind the pulpit, it's relatively easy. But when it is one-on-one, that is a different thing altogether. There is one thing that both Christians and non-Christians have in common: they are both uptight about evangelism. Non-Christians are uptight about being evangelized, and Christians are uptight about evangelizing.

> We need to look past the façade
> and see the empty, lonely, guilty person.

When I was a teenager hanging around in Newport Beach, I would see the Christians walking around, handing out their little gospel tracts. I would lean against a wall, acting like I didn't care, when all the while my heart was saying, "Would you come and talk to me right now?" But the problem was they bought into my tough-guy façade.

They would walk up, sort of thrusting their tracts in my direction, and say, "Here … read this." I would take it and shove it into my pocket, acting as though I did not care. But I never threw one away.

At home I kept a drawer in which I kept all religious literature given to me by any person of any kind of faith whatsoever. Every now and then, I would pull out this drawer, dump it on my bed, and sit there trying to figure out what all this stuff meant. I needed someone to show me the way. I was just waiting for that. That is what most people out there are searching for: someone like you. And again, the primary way we are to share this message is verbally. As 1 Corinthians 1:21 tells us, "For since, in the wisdom of God, the world through wisdom did not know God, it pleased God through the foolishness of the message preached to save those who believe."

Many of us have a hard time separating the sin from the sinner.

Yet many of us give up so easily. We will invite our unbelieving friends to church or a Christian event, and when they say no, we never approach the subject again. My question is do we really believe what we claim we believe—that there really is a heaven and hell, that the wages of sin really are death? If so, how can we be so casual about telling others?

This comes back to the *why* of evangelism. Why should we tell others about Jesus? Because the Lord told us to, and because verbal communication is the primary way that it is done. But that brings me back to an issue I already raised. We should share the gospel because we care. Do you have a burden, a heart for people who do not know the Lord? Sometimes we see them as the enemy rather than people who are trapped by sin. Yet the Bible describes it in a different way:

> A servant of the Lord must not quarrel but must be kind to everyone, be able to teach, and be patient with difficult people. Gently instruct those who oppose the truth. Perhaps God will change those people's hearts, and they will learn the truth. Then they will come to their senses and escape from the devil's trap. For they have been held captive by him to do whatever he wants. (2 Tim. 2:24–26 NLT)

People can tell whether you really care. Many years ago in England, a criminal named Charles Peace was arrested and condemned to death. He had been a burglar, a forger, and also was guilty of double murder. As he was on his way to the gallows, the chaplain who walked by his side mechanically went though his often-repeated speech about the power of Jesus Christ to save from sin. Suddenly Charles Peace stopped, looked at the minister, and said, "Do you believe that? Do you *really* believe that? If I believed that, I would willingly crawl across England on broken glass to tell men it was true."

If we really believe what we believe, then why aren't we doing more to get the message out? Jesus cares about people, and so should we.

The Need for Evangelism

Having looked at the *who, where,* and *why* of evangelism, let's now look at what Jesus tells us about the need for evangelism.

This was a crucial time in Jesus' life and ministry. A new phase had begun. His Galilean ministry was now over, and the long, slow journey to Jerusalem had begun as "He steadfastly set His face to go to Jerusalem" (Luke 9:51). Now to prepare the way, He selected seventy new disciples to go before Him into the various areas where He himself eventually would be going.

> After these things the Lord appointed seventy others also, and sent them two by two before His face into every city and place where He Himself was about to go. Then He said to them, "The harvest truly is great, but the laborers are few; therefore pray the Lord of the harvest to send out laborers into His harvest." (Luke 10:1–2)

From this passage, we can draw direct parallels to our own lives and the times in which we are living. Like these seventy who were preparing the way for Jesus' arrival, we, too, are preparing the way for His return. These are critical, strategic times for sharing the gospel. Jesus used a similar an expression in John 4:35 to what we find here in Luke 10: "Behold, I say to you, lift up your eyes and look at the fields, for *they are already white for harvest!*" (emphasis mine). In these words we see the real heart of God toward this world.

Do you want to know what God is like? Just look at Jesus. Clearly from this passage and others, Jesus cared deeply about people. Matthew's Gospel tells us He was "moved with compassion" for the multitudes (Matt. 9:36; 14:14). Everywhere Jesus went, He was literally mobbed by people who were pushing and pulling, always wanting something from Him. But Jesus saw their deepest need and where they were hurting the most. He saw behind the façades and behind the defense mechanisms and heard the real cry of their hearts. He saw them as sheep without a shepherd, going astray—and He had compassion.

> If we are going to reflect the heart of God, then we have to care about people.

People put up a front and pretend to be happy when they are not. But deep down inside, we are all really the same, with the same hurts and needs. Today, just as in Jesus' day, the fields are "white for harvest." This is true globally as well as nationally.

Billy Graham: Four Universal Truths

When Billy Graham spoke to itinerant evangelists in Amsterdam in 1983, he told them he had found certain things that were true of every culture he had encountered. He said, "When I go out to proclaim the gospel, whether it's a street corner in Nairobi or a meeting in Seoul, Korea, I know there are certain things that are true in the hearts and minds of all people."

First, he said there is an essential emptiness in every life without Christ. All humanity keeps crying for something, but they do not know what it is. Pascal said it well when he stated, "There is a God-shaped vacuum in every life that only God can fill." Romans 8:20 says, "For the creation was subjected to futility, not willingly, but because of Him who subjected it in hope; because the creation itself also will be delivered from the bondage of corruption into the glorious liberty of the children of God."

Second, he said we can assume that in our hearers, there is a loneliness. You can be in a crowd of people, even at a party, and suddenly have a wave of loneliness sweep over you, a sense that you are all alone in this world. It is really a loneliness for God.

Third, he said that people have a sense of guilt. The head of a mental hospital in London said, "I could release half of my patients if I could find a way to rid them of a sense of guilt." The reason people feel guilt is because God has given them a conscience. As Romans 2:15 says, "They demonstrate that God's law is written in their hearts, for their own conscience and thoughts either accuse them or tell them they are doing right" (NLT). Deep inside, we feel guilt, because as the Bible says, "Everyone has sinned; we all fall short of God's glorious standard" (Rom. 3:23 NLT).

Fourth, he said there is a universal fear of death. Death frightens us. It is fear of the unknown. The Bible speaks of "those who through fear of death were all their lifetime subject to bondage" (Heb. 2:15). It has been said there are two unchallengeable things that are true of every person: we all want to be happy, and we're all going to die.

So we need to look past the façade and see the empty, lonely, guilty person. Jesus said, "For the Son of Man has come to seek and to save that which was lost" (Luke 19:10). The word "lost" speaks of something that has value, but is simply broken. Many of us have a hard time separating the sin from the sinner, forgetting that we are to love the sinner and hate the sin. If we are going to reflect the heart of God, then we have to care about people, and specifically unbelieving people. They are not the enemy; they are sheep without a shepherd. And lest we forget, it wasn't all that long ago that you and I were among them.

Thankfully, the Lord reached out, touched us, and brought us to our senses. And without knowing your personal story, I would venture to say that He did that through human instruments, most likely many people who sowed seeds in your life over a number of years. And most likely, it was a single person who articulated the gospel for you when suddenly the lights went on. Thank God for that person! But here is the question: Will you be a person like that for someone else?

What God Values

Souls are of the greatest value to God, and they should be to us as well. When Jesus said, "The harvest truly is great, but the laborers are few" (Luke 10:2), He set forth an idea that the people we are reaching out to have great value in God's sight. Jesus did not compare them to blades of grass, sands of the sea, or dust in the wind, but to ears of corn. Just as corn is valuable to a farmer, the souls of humanity are valuable to God. Jesus looks upon each individual as someone of great value. Of all God's creation, people are the most precious to Him. And He values us so much that He sent His very Son to spill His blood for us. God has said, "Behold, all souls are Mine; the soul of the father as well as the soul of the son is Mine; the soul who sins shall die" (Ezek. 18:4).

> Evangelism is work.
> It can be very difficult at times.

My wife and I were in a restaurant one day when our server told us that she had been dedicated by me as a young girl. I asked her how she was doing spiritually, and she said she was doing well. But when she returned about five minutes later, she told us that some years before, she had an unplanned pregnancy and had made an appointment to have an abortion. But the day before the appointment, she heard one of my messages and changed her mind. She told us that her daughter was now six years old. How I thank God for the decision that young mother made. It's the power of the Word of God.

That is why I preach the gospel and teach the Bible. That is why I do what I do, and why you must do what you can do. That little six-year-old girl will one day grow up, marry, and have children. And her children will have children, each a precious soul to God.

Souls are valuable to God, and His heart yearns for souls to come to Him. From Genesis to Revelation, we see God calling humanity to himself.

Looking for Laborers

Because God has chosen to reach people through people, He is looking for laborers to harvest the crops: "Then He said to them, 'The harvest truly is great, but the laborers are few; *therefore pray the Lord of the harvest to send out laborers into His harvest'* "(Luke 10:2, emphasis mine).

God is looking for laborers—not observers, spectators, or critics, but workers! I am amazed at how critical some people can be about large-scale evangelism like we do in our Harvest Crusades. "I believe in one-on-one evangelism, not 'mass evangelism,' " they will say. Yet Harvest Crusades are about both. One proceeds from the other. And more importantly, both are found in Scripture. What happened with Philip and the Ethiopian dignitary in Acts 8 was personal, or one-on-one, evangelism. And what happened on the day of Pentecost in Acts 2 was mass evangelism.

I came to faith at an open meeting, through what some might call mass evangelism. No one personally invited me to that meeting, and no one had ever taken me aside and shared the gospel with me one-on-one. Even so, I heard the gospel proclaimed at that meeting, and I responded to it.

And my experience is not necessarily unique. At an Anaheim Harvest Crusade a few years ago, one person who made a decision for Christ told his follow-up worker that he was on his way to rob a liquor store that night when he noticed the stadium lights were on. He decided to find out what was going on, came in, heard the gospel, and walked forward at the invitation and committed his life to Jesus Christ!

So do I really believe that all the people who respond to the invitation are truly coming to the Lord? No, I don't. But I also believe there are thousands who do make genuine commitments to Christ. Not only that, but many of them have gone into full-time ministry as pastors and missionaries. I was once at a pastor's conference where I talked to four pastors, independent of one another, who told me they had come to Christ at a Harvest Crusade and were in full-time ministry, planting their own churches and reaching people.

My job, if you will, is to proclaim the gospel to people in a biblical, compassionate, and clear way, while God's job is to convert them. But I do want to use every means at my disposal to do my part well.

I remember reading about a woman who walked up to the great evangelist, D. L. Moody, and said, "Mr. Moody, I don't like the way you do evangelism."

"Well ma'am, I am open to correction," D. L. Moody replied. "Please tell me how do you do evangelism."

She said, "Well, Mr. Moody, I don't."

"Well ma'am," he said, "I like my way of doing it better than your way of not doing it."

Jesus said the laborers are few. A laborer is someone who gets out into the fields and goes to work. And yes, evangelism is work. It can be very difficult at times. But as it's been said, "Without God, man cannot. Without man, God will not."

There can be times when evangelism doesn't seem to be worth the effort. But a farmer could feel the same way when a crop doesn't take, and a fisherman could feel the same way when he doesn't get a single bite. But when your table is filled with food or when you reel in that record-setting fish, it all suddenly becomes worthwhile. When you see a person come to Christ whom you've been praying for, it is all worth it. The Bible says there is joy in heaven over one sinner that comes to repentance (see Luke 15:7), and "Those who sow in tears shall reap in joy. He who continually goes forth weeping, bearing seed for sowing, shall doubtless come again with rejoicing, bringing his sheaves with him" (Psa. 126:5–6).

God is looking for workers.

The people are many, their needs are great, and God wants laborers. But note that Jesus said, "Therefore pray the Lord of the harvest to send out laborers into *His* harvest" (Luke 10:2, emphasis mine). It is *His* harvest, not ours. Many of our attempts at sharing the gospel fail because we do it in our own strength. As I pointed out in the previous chapter, conversion is the work of God and God alone.

In the original language, the phrase "send out" that Jesus used is much more forcible. It means to "push them forward and thrust them out." So this verse could be translated, "Therefore pray the Lord of the harvest to thrust out laborers into His harvest."

Jesus used another important word in this verse: pray. We are to pray for the Lord to raise up laborers for His harvest. But we also must be willing to become laborers ourselves. We all have a part to play.

When we hold a Harvest Crusade, literally hundreds of people help us, from ushering to counseling to praying to bringing someone to the crusade. And that's only naming a few ways people are laboring in the harvest, literally.

How about you? Is God thrusting you out among family and friends? Are you working in the field, or are you sitting in the shade, drinking lemonade?

The harvest is great, but the laborers are few. The observers are many. The critics are many. But the laborers are few.

God is looking for workers. He said, "So I sought for a man among them who would make a wall, and stand in the gap before Me on behalf of the land, that I should not destroy it; but I found no one" (Ezek. 22:30) and "The eyes of the Lord run to and fro throughout the whole earth, to show Himself strong on behalf of those whose heart is loyal to Him" (2 Chron. 16:9).

Will you pray that the Lord would send laborers into the harvest? Will you become a laborer? Will you ask the Holy Spirit to stir your heart to answer the desire and command of Jesus? Will you allow God's Spirit to stir you deeply with a burden for those who are like sheep without a shepherd?

He may call you to cross the ocean as a missionary or to simply cross the street, but He wants you to be a laborer in the harvest. We need to infiltrate and influence our culture, to go into all the world and preach the gospel.

Before we do that, however, we need to know exactly what the gospel is. So let's look at the definition together in the next chapter.

The Three W's of Evangelism

Who is called to "go into all the world?" *We are*. We have been redeemed by Jesus and belong to Him. As our Commander in Chief, He calls us to do this.

Where are we to go? *Everywhere*. We are to go into all our world and preach the gospel—into our neighborhoods, schools, beaches, malls … everywhere.

Why are we to do this? *Because God has primarily chosen to reach people through people*, and we need to genuinely care for lost people.

3 The "What" of Evangelism: the Gospel

On May 15, 2006, British mountaineer David Sharp died near the summit of Mount Everest in a rocky cave. It was his third attempt to scale the world's highest mountain, and media reports speculated whether he reached the top. But the irony of his tragic story is that while the blood in his arms and legs was turning to ice, a possible forty-two people passed Sharp that morning on their way to the summit—people who could have saved him. Some looked the other way, while a few paused long enough to hear him say, "My name is David Sharp. I'm with Asian Trekking. ... " Upon hearing of Sharp's death, one climber cold-heartedly remarked, "We know the risk. People die on Everest every year." When the media later picked up on comments by the climber, no less than Sir Edmund Hillary, the first climber ever to summit Everest, strongly criticized those who hadn't helped Sharp, reportedly calling their actions "despicable." Before he left on his trip, Sharp had assured his mother, "You are never on your own. There are climbers everywhere."[3]

> God can and will use you
> to bring others into His kingdom.

That tragedy on Everest sounded a lot like a modern version of Jesus' parable of the Good Samaritan. But it also sounds like some Christians who are so busy on their way up to the summit that they bypass lost people without so much as a twinge of concern. They watch them slowly die, or worse, never even notice them to begin with.

Jesus always had time for individuals, patiently engaging, conversing, loving, and winning them to faith. All of us as believers have been called to do this as well.

The word "gospel" has largely lost its meaning in today's culture.

So far, we've learned that Jesus has given us, His people, our marching orders to "go into all the world and preach the gospel to every creature" (Mark 16:15). Yet in all honesty, many—if not most of us—are not following His command. Why is that? I hear believers citing reasons such as a feeling of inadequacy or lack of skill when it comes to sharing the gospel. Others are afraid of failure and how people will respond. Those are valid concerns, by the way. In the pages that follow, I want to help you overcome those concerns and realize that God can and will use you to bring others into His kingdom. Granted, not every Christian is called as an evangelist, but we are all called to evangelize. We are called to share the gospel.

What Is the Gospel?

"Gospel" is a word we hear tossed around a lot today. We call a certain style of music "gospel," designated as such because of the particular sound it has. When we want someone to believe what we're telling them, we say, "It's the gospel truth!" We hear people say they are "preaching the gospel," when, in reality, they don't seem to know what the term means. Sadly, the word "gospel" has largely lost its meaning in today's culture.

It is my belief that most Americans, not to mention the rest of the world, have not really heard the gospel. For that matter, I think there may be a surprising number of people in the church who actually don't know what the gospel message really is.

What is the gospel? What elements must it include for it to be accurate? Are there "false gospels" we must be aware of? You might be thinking, *I'll leave that to you pastors and theologians to figure out. All I know is that I'm already saved and going to heaven.*

But we all need to know what the gospel is for two very important reasons:

1. We want to make sure we have heard the true gospel and have responded to it, lest we have a false hope concerning a salvation we think we have. Our very eternal destiny hangs on it.

2. Jesus commanded us to "go into all the world and preach the gospel." His words were not merely addressed to pastors, teachers, evangelists, and missionaries. They are addressed to every follower of Jesus Christ. We cannot be disengaged or disinterested in this subject, because the literal eternal destinies of people hang in the balance.

Beware of Counterfeits

What would you think of a surgeon who just started cutting away on a patient without really knowing what he or she was doing? One mistake and the patient could be disabled for life or even killed. Yet this message we bring has even more far-reaching consequences than these, because there are eternal ramifications.

Yet so many will be careless in this area by offering God's forgiveness without any mention of repentance or by presenting Jesus Christ as though He were a mere additive to make one's life a little better and more successful. This is not the true gospel. And it can give false hope.

> We as Christians are to rightly divide the word of truth.

On the other extreme, some offer a rule-laden or over-complex gospel by telling people they must do certain things or look a certain way to be saved. This robs the gospel of its simplicity and power—and it also imposes false guilt.

This is why the Bible reminds us that we as Christians are to rightly divide the word of truth (see 2 Tim. 2:15). It also tells us to "watch your life and doctrine closely. Persevere in them, because if you do, you will save both yourself and your hearers" (1 Tim. 4:16 NIV).

Some Christians might say, "I'm not into doctrine. I just love Jesus!" That is a sweet sentiment, but Christians who embrace it might end up loving the wrong Jesus. C. S. Lewis gave this warning, "If you do not listen to theology, that will not mean that you have no ideas about God. It will mean that you have a lot of wrong ones—bad, muddled, out-of-date ideas."[4]

We must be careful, therefore, to accurately present the gospel, meaning that certain elements must be in place, because there is also a false, counterfeit gospel. Paul wrote to the churches of Galatia,

> I am astonished that you are so quickly deserting the one who called you by the grace of Christ and are turning to a different gospel—which is really no gospel at all. Evidently some people are throwing you into confusion and are trying to pervert the gospel of Christ. But even if we or an angel from heaven should preach a gospel other than the one we preached to you, let him be eternally condemned! (Gal. 1:6–8 NIV)

The Good News and the Bad News

So let's explore together the elements that must be present for the gospel to be the gospel. A technical definition of the word "gospel" is "good news." We've all heard the expression, "I have some good news and some bad news. … " And when it comes to sharing the gospel, we must present the good news and the bad news.

A technical definition of the word "gospel" is "good news."

The bad news is the fact that we all stand as sinners before a holy God. No matter who we are, we have all sinned—sometimes in ignorance and often on purpose. The Bible tells us that "all have sinned and fall short of the glory of God" (Rom. 3:23) and that "if we say that we have no sin, we deceive ourselves, and the truth is not in us" (1 John 1:8). God has given us His law, the Ten Commandments, not to make us righteous, but to show us that we all fall miserably short.

They are like a moral mirror that shows us our flaws and sin. They shut our mouths and open our eyes.

Often when I'm sharing the gospel, I will go over a few of the Ten Commandments and ask, "Have you ever broken any of these commandments? Ever stolen, lied, or taken God's name in vain? The Bible says, 'For whoever keeps the whole law and yet stumbles at just one point is guilty of breaking all of it' " (James 2:10 NIV). The point of all this is to show that everyone needs Jesus. Everyone has sinned, and no one is good enough to get into heaven.

Yet this idea of all humanity being utterly sinful is very hard for many people to stomach. They believe in the innate goodness of man. But as the Scripture says, "God looks down from heaven upon the children of men, to see if there are any who understand, who seek God. Every one of them has turned aside; they have together become corrupt; there is none who does good, no, not one" (Ps. 53:2–3).

This does not mean that humanity is not capable of commendable things. There are people who are great humanitarians or heroes. The soldier who throws himself on the grenade to protect his buddies is a great hero. A person who helps the hurting is good in the sense of human kindness. So to say, "There is none who does good, no, not one," does not mean there is no good in people, but that there is no good in people that can satisfy God.

God is holy, and He requires holiness from us. Hebrews 12:14 tells us, "Pursue peace with all people, and holiness, without which no one will see the Lord." And we are told in 1 Peter 1:15–16, "But as He who called you is holy, you also be holy in all your conduct, because it is written, 'Be holy, for I am holy.' "

I read about a man named Fred Turner who, a number of years ago, set out walking across America to prove that most people are good. He made it only as far as the Georgia-South Carolina state line when he was robbed and pushed off a bridge. According to Turner, a faded, red pickup truck pulled next to him while he was walking across a bridge. "They asked me if I was the guy walking across America," he said. "I told them yes, and they said, 'Good. Give me your wallet.' " Then they pushed him. He dropped off the bridge, falling 75 to 100 feet. "This could've happened two months from now and I wouldn't feel so bad," Turner commented. "I only got through one state!"

Only One Resolution

Humanity is not basically good; we are basically bad. Very bad. But just as a jeweler will display a beautiful ring or necklace against a dark velvet background to accentuate its beauty, God has sought to show us just how good the Good News is by first telling us the bad news. Seeing our complete weakness, our inability to do anything whatsoever to alleviate our miserable condition, God did the ultimate for us:

> When we were utterly helpless, Christ came at just the right time and died for us sinners. Now, most people would not be willing to die for an upright person, though someone might perhaps be willing to die for a person who is especially good. But God showed his great love for us by sending Christ to die for us while we were still sinners. (Rom. 5:6–8 NLT)

Because there was no other way to satisfy the righteous demands of God, because of our inability to improve ourselves (much less save ourselves), because we faced a future in hell because of our sin, God, in His great love, sent His own Son to come down from heaven and die on the cross in our very place. Paul personalized this great act of mercy by saying, "I have been crucified with Christ; it is no longer I who live, but Christ lives in me; and the life which I now live in the flesh I live by faith in the Son of God, who loved me and gave Himself for me" (Gal. 2:20).

Humanity is not basically good;
we are basically bad.

There was no other way to resolve this serious sin issue we all face. We know that God is perfect. We know that humanity is imperfect and sinful. So Jesus, the God-man, was uniquely qualified to bridge the gap between sinful humanity and a holy God. He was the only one who could ever do that.

As 2 Corinthians 5:18–19 tells us,

> And all of this is a gift from God, who brought us back to himself through Christ. And God has given us this task of reconciling people to him. For God was in Christ, reconciling the world to himself, no longer counting people's sins against them. And he gave us this wonderful message of reconciliation. (NLT)

It is not about what we did to please or reach God. We did everything to displease Him and fail to reach Him. Instead, "all of this is a gift from God, who brought us back to himself through Christ. … " This is why Jesus Christ is the only way to the Father. Jesus himself said it: "I am the way, the truth, and the life. No one comes to the Father except through Me" (John 14:6). Peter echoed those words as he stood before the Sanhedrin: "Nor is there salvation in any other, for there is no other name under heaven given among men by which we must be saved" (Acts 4:12). Paul said the same thing: "For there is one God and one Mediator between God and men, the Man Christ Jesus" (1 Tim. 2:5). For us as Christians to say anything else is wrong—and a misrepresentation of the gospel.

There on the cross, all the sin of the world was poured upon Jesus Christ as He became the sin sacrifice for us: "For He made Him who knew no sin to be sin for us, that we might become the righteousness of God in Him" (2 Cor. 5:21). At the cross, Jesus took the penalty for every sin we have ever committed.

In the movie, *The Last Emperor,* the young child who was anointed the last emperor of China lives a life of incredible luxury with one thousand servants at his command. His brother asks him, "What happens when you do wrong?"

"When I do wrong," the boy emperor responds, "someone else is punished." To demonstrate, he breaks a jar, and one of his servants is beaten.

With the gospel, the very opposite is the case. Jesus reversed that ancient pattern: when the servants erred, the King was punished. Grace is free only because the Giver himself has borne the cost.

The Essential Gospel Message

In 1 Corinthians 15:1–4, Paul gives a simple summation of the gospel:

> Now, brothers, I want to remind you of *the gospel I preached to you,* which you received and on which you have taken your stand. *By this gospel you are saved,* if you hold firmly to the word I preached to you. Otherwise, you have believed in vain. For what I received I passed on to you as of first importance: that *Christ died for our sins* according to the Scriptures, that *he was buried,* that *he was raised on the third day according to the Scriptures.* (NIV, emphasis mine)

The gospel, in a nutshell, is: Christ died for our sins, was buried, and was raised on the third day. Imbed that thought deeply into your mind. There are other elements, but this is the cornerstone—the death and resurrection of Jesus Christ. Someone once asked C. H. Spurgeon if he could put his Christian faith into a few words. He answered, "It is all in four words: Jesus died for me."

> Grace is free only because the
> Giver himself has borne the cost.

Consider the fact that the apostle Paul was a brilliant orator and communicator. He was deeply schooled in biblical law as well as in the wisdom of Greece. If anyone could have leaned on his intellect, it would have been Paul. Yet it is amazing to read accounts in the Book of Acts of his sharing the gospel with powerful government leaders and realize that he kept it so simple. Paul emphasized the importance of this simplicity again and again in his writings:

> For Christ did not send me to baptize, but to preach the gospel—not with words of human wisdom, lest the cross of Christ be emptied of its power. (1 Cor. 1:17 NIV)

> When I came to you, brothers, I did not come with eloquence or superior wisdom as I proclaimed to you the testimony about God. For I resolved to know nothing while I was with you except Jesus Christ and him crucified. (1 Cor. 2:1 NIV)

Typically, Paul began with his personal testimony. Then he would always key in on what happened when Jesus died on the cross. That is the pattern that we, too, should follow.

Of course there are hard questions that unbelievers can fire at us. But we need to know that the essence of the gospel message is the cross. If you were to simply use the information I have just shared with you, then you would have enough to be spiritually dangerous and to make an impact for the kingdom of God.

We often underestimate the raw power of the gospel for reaching even the most hardened heart. Yet Paul said, "For the message of the cross is foolishness to those who are perishing, but to us who are being saved it is the power of God" (1 Cor. 1:18) and "I am not ashamed of the gospel of Christ, for it is the power of God to salvation for everyone who believes" (Rom. 1:16). Paul was reminding us there is a distinct power in the simple message of the life, words, death, and resurrection of Jesus Christ from the dead.

So the gospel is simply this: The message that we are all separated from God because of our sin, and the result of this sin is an emptiness, an ever-present guilt, and a certain fear of death. But because God loved us in spite of our rebellion, He sent His own Son to die in our place and bridge the gap between Him and us.

Don't underestimate the gospel's appeal. Don't be ashamed of its simplicity. Don't add to it or take away from it. Just proclaim it and then stand back and watch what God will do.

I have been preaching the gospel for more than three decades now, and I have been amazed time and time again at how God so powerfully uses this simple yet incredibly profound message to radically change lives, from satanists to religious people, from broken families and drug addicts to those deceived by the cults. Praise God for the gospel!

The Conversion Process

Having learned what the gospel is, what is the appropriate response to it? How do we enter into a relationship with God? Matthew 11:28–30 provides the answer: "Come to Me, all you who labor and are heavy laden, and I will give you rest.

Take My yoke upon you and learn from Me, for I am gentle and lowly in heart, and you will find rest for your souls. For My yoke is easy and My burden is light."

In these verses, Jesus gives three steps that define the process of entering into and enjoying a relationship with God:

1. Come to Me.

2. Take My yoke upon you.

3. Learn from Me.

First, we must come to Him. We come to Him with all our problems, sins, and shortcomings. We respond to His invitation with the assurance that He said, "The one who comes to Me I will by no means cast out" (John 6:37). Conversion is not some long, drawn-out process. It is immediate, instantaneous. Thinking about it is not enough. When the prodigal son was in a distant country, he knew he needed to return home. But thinking about it and doing it are two different things. That is why, when we share the gospel, we should always give people the opportunity to come to Christ. Much evangelism does not go beyond getting a nibble, because we don't throw the net.

Of course, there is a right time and a wrong time to do this. First, we want to make sure the people we are talking to have understood the essential gospel message. Going over the facts, we must let them know what the gospel is, and what it is to believe. Then they must understand that to come to Christ, they must believe in and receive Him as both Lord and Savior. They must be willing to confess and turn from their sin, as 1 John 1:9 says: "If we confess our sins, He is faithful and just to forgive us our sins and to cleanse us from all unrighteousness." And they must believe in Jesus, as John 3:16 says: "For God so loved the world that He gave His only begotten Son, that whoever *believes in Him* should not perish but have everlasting life" (emphasis mine).

The Role of Repentance

The second step is "take My yoke upon You." This concept would have been readily understood by the people of Jesus' day, but it is largely lost on us. The idea is that of being "yoked" to Jesus, meaning that we make a decision to come under His direction for our lives. There is no such thing as having Christ as Savior, but not as Lord. We give Him the steering wheel of our lives, so to speak. My family could tell you that I am the worst backseat driver. I like to be in control of the car. But Jesus is saying to us, "I want the steering wheel, and I don't need your advice." Many have their own plans for their lives and ask the Lord to come along for the ride. They may even have a little bumper sticker on their car that says, "God is my copilot." But God does not want to be their copilot. In fact, He doesn't even want them in the cockpit. Jesus wants to control our lives, and that is actually a wonderful thing.

> Don't underestimate the gospel's appeal.

Imagine being in a car that is careening out of control, when Jeff Gordon offers to take the wheel. Even with my strong affinity for backseat driving, I would gladly turn over the wheel to him. Why? Because I know that he is a seasoned NASCAR driver, and the odds of getting control of that car are much better with him behind the wheel.

Jesus offers to take control of our lives. But we must first admit that we are helpless sinners in desperate need of a Savior. We must be ready to put our trust and faith in Jesus from that time forward, which means to turn the direction of our lives over to Him. In the process, we turn away from our old, sinful lifestyles and are willing to change and become different people. In short, we need to repent. Peter preached, "Repent therefore and be converted, that your sins may be blotted out, so that times of refreshing may come from the presence of the Lord" (Acts 3:19). And the prophet Isaiah said, "Seek the Lord while He may be found, call upon Him while He is near.

Let the wicked forsake his way, and the unrighteous man his thoughts; let him return to the Lord, and He will have mercy on him; and to our God, for He will abundantly pardon" (Isa. 55:6–7).

Belief and repentance are but two sides of the same coin. To believe is to take hold of something, and to repent is to let go of something. Paul brought both ideas together in Acts 20:21: "Testifying to Jews, and also to Greeks, repentance toward God and faith toward our Lord Jesus Christ."

Repentance means more than merely feeling regret or sorrow. We may feel sorry for sin, especially if we reap the consequences of it. The person caught in a lie is sorry. The criminal who gets caught is sorry. The teenage girl who finds out she is pregnant outside of marriage is sorry. But does this sorrow lead to change? Not if the person caught in a lie determines to be more careful next time. Not if the criminal plots his next crime with more foresight. Not if the teenage girl will try to have only "safe sex" from now on.

Repentance means a change of mind and a confession of wrongdoing. It means to turn around, to change one's direction, and to change both the mind and will. It does not denote just any change, but always a change from wrong to right, away from sin to righteousness. Remorse is being sorry, while repentance is being sorry enough to stop. Jesus commanded, "Produce fruit in keeping with repentance" (Luke 3:8 NIV).

> Belief and repentance are
> but two sides of the same coin.

The recognition of personal sin must always be the first step in repentance. But to stop there can be useless at best and dangerous at worst. The problem with recognizing personal sin without taking action can be self-deceiving, because it causes one to think that mere acknowledgement is all that is necessary.

An insincere King Saul confessed his sin (see 1 Sam. 15:24), but that didn't stop him from his collision course with judgment. The rich young ruler who asked Jesus how to have eternal life went away sorrowful, but not repentant (see Luke 18:23). Even Judas Iscariot was sorrowful over his betrayal of Jesus (see Matt. 27:4). All of these men recognized their sin, yet none of them repented.

Paul put it succinctly when he defined salvation: " 'To *open their eyes,* in order to *turn them from darkness to light,* and *from the power of Satan to God,* that they may *receive forgiveness of sins and an inheritance* among those who are sanctified by faith in Me' " (Acts 26:18, emphasis mine). So we must turn from sin and turn to Christ by faith.

When I am preaching, I often sum up my messages with the following points:

1. Realize you are a sinner.

2. Recognize Christ died for you.

3. Repent of your sins.

4. Receive Christ as Savior and Lord.

Becoming New

We've learned that we must come to Him. We must take His yoke upon us. And the next step in the process is to learn from Him. As we walk and talk with Jesus Christ in our hearts and lives and begin to read His Word, we will see things with new eyes, because we are new people.

The only way to tell whether a conversion has taken place is to look for results. Two of those results will be a hatred for sin and a love for God's Word. The Bible says, "But whoever keeps His word, truly the love of God is perfected in him. By this we know that we are in Him" (1 John 2:5).

In 1 John, we find four earmarks of a true conversion.

1. *Confession of Jesus as Lord:* "Whoever confesses that Jesus is the Son of God, God abides in him, and he in God" (1 John 4:15).

2. *Unhappiness or misery over personal sin:* "No one who is born of God will continue to sin, because God's seed remains in him; he cannot go on sinning, because he has been born of God" (1 John 3:9 NIV). From the original language, the phrase "will continue to sin" could be translated, "does not habitually sin."

3. *Fellowship with other believers:* "Everyone who believes that Jesus is the Christ is born of God, and everyone who loves the father loves his child as well" (1 John 5:1 NIV); and "These people left our churches, but they never really belonged with us; otherwise they would have stayed with us. When they left, it proved that they did not belong with us" (1 John 2:19 NLT).

4. *Obedience to Christ's commands:* "This is love for God: to obey his commands. And his commands are not burdensome" (1 John 5:3 NIV).

How Will They Hear?

One of His commands, we've learned so far, is to "go into all the world and preach the gospel." My question for you is when is the last time you told someone about Jesus Christ? Romans 10:14 says, "How then shall they call on Him in whom they have not believed? And how shall they believe in Him of whom they have not heard? And how shall they hear without a preacher?"

There are people right now who are waiting for you, Christian, to show them the way. As we make our way up the summit, let's not forget those along the way, those people who are waiting for someone to reach out to them and help them with the only message that can change their eternal destiny: the gospel of Jesus Christ. Will you do that? Will you be available for God to use you?

The Essential Gospel

Christ died for our sins, was buried, and was raised on the third day.

4 Practical Effects of Salvation

As we are seeking to share the gospel message with others, there are some biblical concepts we need to first grasp so that we have the big picture.

Two key terms we must know and understand are "justification" and "sanctification." So important are these terms that I would say that understanding them can and will impact your Christian experience. So don't let these words put you off. You need to know what they mean and how they practically apply to you. These are the results of conversion.

Justification

C. H. Spurgeon said, "It is admitted by all evangelical Christians that the standing or falling in the church is that of justification by faith." So what does it mean to be justified before God?

The word "justified" carries a twofold meaning. First, it speaks of the forgiveness of all your sins. This simply means that the day you put your faith in Jesus Christ as Savior and Lord is the day that all of your sins were instantaneously forgiven and removed. Have you ever done anything that you are ashamed of? If you have repented of that sin and have turned your back on it, then the Bible clearly declares that you are forgiven.

Forgiven and Forgotten

Speaking of our sins, God says, "For I will forgive their iniquity, and their sin I will remember no more" (Jer. 31:34). And in Micah we find these encouraging words:

> Who is a God like You, pardoning iniquity and passing over
> the transgression of the remnant of His heritage? He does
> not retain His anger forever, because He delights in mercy.

He will again have compassion on us, and will subdue our iniquities. You will cast all our sins into the depths of the sea. (Micah 7:18–19)

Have you ever lost anything in a lake or the ocean? It is pretty much a lost cause. Once it goes down, it goes way down. God has taken your sin and has thrown it into the deepest part of the sea. Simply translated, it is gone. Therefore, we should not choose to remember what God has chosen to forget. As Corrie ten Boom said, "God has taken our sins, cast them into the sea of forgetfulness, and posted a sign that says, 'No fishing allowed.' "

The Ultimate Deal

But that is only one part of justification. Justification is more than just forgiveness. If all justification consisted of were forgiveness, then I would venture to say that it's the greatest deal ever offered to humanity. But justification not only speaks of what God has taken away; it also speaks of what He has put in its place. The word "justified" means to have something placed to your credit. The Greek word describing this process is used eleven times in Romans 4. It is translated by the English verbs "account," "count," and "impute." It means to put to one's account. Romans 4:5 tells us, "But to him who does not work but believes on Him who justifies the ungodly, his faith is accounted for righteousness."

> We should not choose to remember
> what God has chosen to forget.

So we see that justification is more than what God has done for us: forgiveness and the removal of guilt and the condemnation that accompanied it. Justification is also what God has given us.

Justification is a legal act of God, declaring the sinner guiltless before God. It is a complete acquittal. When God justifies us, He does so by placing the righteousness of Christ into our account.

That balances the moral and spiritual budget for us. As Paul said, "I no longer count on my own righteousness through obeying the law; rather, I become righteous through faith in Christ. For God's way of making us right with himself depends on faith" (Phil. 3:9 NLT).

This is not a gradual process. It is instantaneous. It is immediate. That is what God has done for us through justification. He forgave us of all of the wrongs we have done. He removed our sins. And now He has put Christ's righteousness into our account.

> ## Living a sanctified life is working out what God has worked in.

Sanctification

So having experienced justification *positionally*, we experience sanctification *practically*. Sanctification means being "set apart." That is, set apart to be used by God and to become more like Christ:

> But in a great house there are not only vessels of gold and silver, but also of wood and clay, some for honor and some for dishonor. Therefore if anyone cleanses himself from the latter, he will be a vessel for honor, *sanctified* and useful for the Master, prepared for every good work. (2 Timothy 2:20–21, emphasis mine)

Living a sanctified life is working out what God has worked in. Sanctification is a part of the whole process of the new birth. In fact, D. L. Moody used six words to describe it:

1. Repentance—a change of mind. A new mind about God.
2. Conversion—a change of life. A new life from God.
3. Regeneration—a change of nature. A new heart from God.
4. Justification—a change of state. A new standing before God.
5. Adoption—a change of family. A new relationship toward God.
6. Sanctification—a change of service. A new condition with God.

A License to Sin?

So, having learned what God has done for us through justification and sanctification as part of the process of new birth, this brings us to a question: Can you really be a genuine child of God, yet continue to live a sinful lifestyle?

In Romans 6, Paul refuted a similar argument he was anticipating from the religious leaders of his day who would think that because he was teaching that salvation comes totally and completely from God and there is nothing we can do to earn it, then it stands to reason that we should keep sinning so that more of God's grace may come. After all, won't God forgive us?

Obviously, this is not what Paul was teaching. One thing we often forget is that although there is forgiveness of sin, there are still repercussions. We sometimes confuse God's leniency with God's approval. We think because we have committed a sin and have not paid an immediate price for it, that somehow God doesn't mind. If a believer sins, but truly repents, that doesn't mean there still cannot be very strong ramifications.

> We sometimes confuse God's leniency with God's approval.

This certainly was the case with David. After he confessed to committing murder to cover up his adulterous relationship with Bathsheba, the prophet Nathan said to him, "The Lord also has put away your sin; you shall not die. However, because by this deed you have given great occasion to the enemies of the Lord to blaspheme, the child also who is born to you shall surely die" (2 Sam. 12:13–14).

Scripture is clear about this: "Do not be deceived, God is not mocked; for whatever a man sows, that he will also reap" (Gal. 6:7). For example, if you were to rob a bank, get caught by the authorities, and then repent before God and say you're sorry, God would forgive you. But you still would go to jail.

The problem with the religious people of Paul's day was that they were putting the cart before the horse. They believed that holy living, which to them meant keeping rules and regulations, brought about God's favor and therefore resulted in salvation. But Paul showed that because of the extensiveness of our sinful condition, there is no way we could earn God's approval. We all fail miserably and continually.

God's favor toward us comes not on the basis of what we've done for Him, but on the basis of what He's done for us. So holy living (which we are incapable of to begin with) will not produce salvation. But salvation will produce holy living.

Justification is not a license to sin, but an incentive to obey.

The teaching of justification is not a license to sin, but an incentive to obey. "No one who is born of God will continue to sin, because God's seed remains in him; he cannot go on sinning, because he has been born of God" (1 John 3:9 NIV).

In Romans 6, the repetition of the word "know" in verses 6 and 9 indicates that Paul wanted us to understand a basic doctrine:

> For we *know* that our old self was crucified with him so that the body of sin might be done away with, that we should no longer be slaves to sin. … For we *know* that since Christ was raised from the dead, he cannot die again; death no longer has mastery over him. (NIV, emphasis mine)

Many would think the way to overcome sin is to say, "No! No!" But Paul's method for overcoming it was by teaching, "Know! Know!" Christian living depends on Christian learning. Duty is always founded on doctrine. If Satan can keep Christians ignorant, then he can keep them impotent. We are often defeated in day-to-day living, because we do not fully realize how much God has placed in our spiritual bank account. It would be like trying to hold back the enemy in a battle without any ammunition, while all the time having more than could ever be used in a thousand battles. Our defeat lies largely in the ignorance of the facts.

There is in Jesus Christ the power to no longer be under sin's control and to live a new life. That power is not the result of imitation. We cannot avoid sin's power merely by imitating Christ. Nor is there power in the repetition of certain phrases. Even prayer itself is not all that is required. The power is not through imitation, but through impartation.

This is a revolutionary concept. It is not trying to humanly live a divine life, but it is to divinely live a human life. It is appropriating the divine provision that God has for us. It is finding and using the ammunition. It is possessing our possessions, just as it was with the children of Israel who had to take possession of their land:

> "Moses My servant is dead. Now therefore, arise, go over this Jordan, you and all this people, to the land which I am giving to them—the children of Israel. Every place that the sole of your foot will tread upon I have given you, as I said to Moses. From the wilderness and this Lebanon as far as the great river, the River Euphrates, all the land of the Hittites, and to the Great Sea toward the going down of the sun, shall be your territory. (Josh. 1:2–3)

All the land was theirs *positionally*, but they still had to take possession of it *practically*. It wasn't always easy, but it was doable. In the same way, we can stand around and admire these principles of justification and sanctification. *Isn't it great what God has given to us?* But do we put them into practice? The answer, many times, is no.

Christian living depends on Christian learning.

Justification by faith is not simply a legal matter between us and God; it is a living relationship. It is justification that brings life (see Rom. 5:18). We are in Christ, identified with Him. Therefore, whatever happened to Christ happened to us. When He died, we died. When He rose, we rose with Him. And we are now seated in "heavenly places" with Him as well (see Eph. 2:1–10).

Because of this living union with Jesus, we also have a totally new relationship to sin. Therefore, many times when believers are "praying for victory," they are missing an essential truth that could revolutionize their spiritual life: we don't fight *for* victory; we fight *from* victory. So we don't fight the devil in our own strength. We stand in the Lord and in the power of His might. We share in what He has done on our behalf. We stand in the finished work of the cross.

The Choice Is Ours

So the question arises: "Shall we continue in sin that grace may abound?" (Rom. 6:1). In the original language, the word "continue" carries the idea of habitual persistence. It was sometimes used to describe a person's purposely living in a certain place and making it his permanent residence.

One summer, I had the opportunity to spend a few days in Nantucket, a beautiful place on the East Coast of the United States. I had never visited anywhere quite like it. We especially enjoyed walking along, looking at the different houses. To provide a sense of continuity and uniformity on the island, there are only five shades of paint that people can use on their homes, all of which appear to be basically gray. There is dark gray, medium gray, and light gray.

As my son Jonathan and I were taking pictures, we found this one, dilapidated house, built partly over the water. There were nets hanging off the walls and junk piled here and there. The windows were broken, and the front door was hanging by one hinge. I thought this house would make a great photo. And I was certain that no one lived there. So I climbed up on the little deck, steadied myself, and told Jonathan to take a picture. Then I went into the house and popped out the doorway. Just as Jonathan was ready to take the next shot, a woman in the back of the house yelled at me and told me to get out! I have to admit, she gave me a start. We got out of there quickly. I couldn't believe this woman actually lived in this place. For that matter, I could not believe that anyone would be allowed to live there, because it looked like the house could come crashing down at any moment.

It reminded me of how a person purposely lives in a state of sin. That woman lived in this dangerous environment and chose to live there, just as some people choose to live in sin. Paul was asking, "How shall those whose relationship to sin has been broken by their dying still be walking and living in sin?" That should be our past, not our present. As Paul wrote to the believers in Ephesus,

> And you He made alive, who were dead in trespasses and sins, in which you once walked according to the course of this world, according to the prince of the power of the air, the spirit who now works in the sons of disobedience, among whom also we all once conducted ourselves in the lusts of our flesh, fulfilling the desires of the flesh and of the mind, and were by nature children of wrath, just as the others. (Eph. 2:1–3)

Our defeat lies largely in the ignorance of the facts.

The word "course" in verse 2 was a word used for a weathervane that blows whatever way the wind does. We once walked "according to the course of this world," Paul was saying, but that has all changed. Now we are "a new creation; old things have passed away; behold, all things have become new" (2 Cor. 5:17).

That is not to say we will not struggle with sin and temptation to some degree throughout the Christian life. The Bible is clear in pointing out that "if we say that we have no sin, we deceive ourselves, and the truth is not in us" (1 John 1:8). When Paul asked, "Shall we continue in sin that grace may abound?" he was not speaking of a believer's occasional falling into sin, because that happens to every believer. Paul was speaking of intentional, willful sinning as an established pattern of life.

However, if there has been no change in a person's lifestyle after conversion, and if he or she continues in sin, the question is not so much whether that person can lose his or her salvation, but whether that person was ever truly converted. Perhaps he or she never really heard the true gospel to begin with.

I would even suggest that many who claim to be Christians really are not. They may have had their eyes opened, but they have never really turned "from darkness to light, and from the power of Satan to God" (Acts 26:18). Commentator Donald Grey Barnhouse said, "Holiness starts where justification finishes, and if holiness does not start, we have the right to suspect that justification never started either."

Paul's answer to the question of whether we should continue in sin was, "Certainly not! How shall we who died to sin live any longer in it?" (Rom. 6:2). He was referring to the position we have. Just as Jesus was crucified and then rose again from the dead, we have done the same, because we are positionally in Christ. We are dead to sin. In other words, when Jesus died, we died with Him to sin. Paul went on to illustrate this idea:

> Or do you not know that as many of us as were baptized into Christ Jesus were baptized into His death? Therefore we were buried with Him through baptism into death, that just as Christ was raised from the dead by the glory of the Father, even so we also should walk in newness of life. (vv. 3–4)

In the context of what Paul was saying, we as believers have made a break with the past. We are dead and buried in our identification with the death and burial of Jesus Christ.

We don't fight for victory; we fight from victory.

What Baptism Means

We have a symbol of that identification in water baptism. Many misunderstand the meaning and purpose of baptism. Water baptism is an outward showing of an inward doing, just as wearing a wedding ring is an outward symbol of what happened on that person's wedding day. Baptism does not wash away one's sins any more than simply putting on a wedding ring makes one married. Baptism is a symbol of identifying with the death and resurrection of Jesus Christ. Some think it is a ritual that plays a role in finding salvation, which is why they will have their babies baptized as a type of dedication.

I am all for infant dedication, but I am not for infant baptism. Why? Quite simply because there is no precedent for it in Scripture. Two requirements are necessary for baptism to be meaningful.

1. *Repentance.* We must repent. Peter told those present at Pentecost, "*Repent,* and let every one of you *be baptized in the name of Jesus Christ* for the remission of sins ... " (Acts 2:38, emphasis mine).

2. *Belief in the Lord Jesus Christ.* We must believe in Jesus Christ as the Son of God. As Philip talked with the Ethiopian dignitary on the road from Jerusalem to Gaza, the dignitary said to him, " 'See, here is water. What hinders me from being baptized?' Then Philip said, 'If you believe with all your heart, you may.' And he answered and said, 'I believe that Jesus Christ is the Son of God' " (Acts 8:36–37). So they went down into the water, and Philip baptized him.

Baptism represents saying goodbye to your old life.

Baptism represents saying goodbye to your old life. Paul raised the question, "Or do you not know that as many of us as were baptized into Christ Jesus were baptized into His death?" (Rom. 6:3). Baptism is the only truly happy funeral service you ever attend. I read about a chaplain during Operation Desert Storm who had to come up with an alternative for baptizing the many American soldiers who were coming to Christ and asking to be baptized. Because there was no actual body of water available in the desert, the chaplain baptized the soldiers in a coffin that had been filled with water. In all reality, it was a more-than-appropriate way to baptize, due to its symbolism.

So does a person have to be baptized to be saved? No. But if a person is saved, then he or she certainly should be baptized. The Bible commands us to do this, and it is even a part of the Great Commission: "Go therefore and make disciples of all the nations, *baptizing* them in the name of the Father and of the Son and of the Holy Spirit ... " (Matt. 28:19, emphasis mine).

But as important as baptism is, it is not a prerequisite for salvation. Some proponents of "baptismal regeneration" cite Mark 16:16, which says, "He who believes and is baptized will be saved; but he who does not believe will be condemned." But notice this verse *does not* say, "He who does not believe *and is not baptized* will be condemned." The emphasis in that verse is on believing and on what should naturally follow. The emphasis is not on baptism.

> As important as baptism is,
> it is not a prerequisite for salvation.

If baptism were a requirement for salvation, then what about the thief on the cross who said to Jesus, "Lord, remember me when You come into Your kingdom"? Jesus didn't insist that he first be baptized. Instead, Jesus told him, "Assuredly, I say to you, today you will be with Me in Paradise" (Luke 2:43).

When Peter was preaching the gospel to some Gentiles and the Holy Spirit came upon them, Peter asked, "Can anyone keep these people from being baptized with water? They have received the Holy Spirit just as we have" (Acts 10:47 NIV). Clearly these people already believed and were empowered by the Holy Spirit before they were baptized.

A New Beginning

Baptism is a symbol of new life in Christ, and the Bible is full of descriptions of the believer's new spiritual life. In Ezekiel, God promises a new heart: "I will give you a new heart and put a new spirit within you; I will take the heart of stone out of your flesh and give you a heart of flesh" (Ezek. 36:26).

The psalmist speaks of a new song: "He has put a new song in my mouth—praise to our God" (Ps. 40:3).

And Ephesians emphasizes a new nature: "Throw off your old sinful nature and your former way of life, which is corrupted by lust and deception. Instead, let the Spirit renew your thoughts and attitudes. Put on your new nature, created to be like God—truly righteous and holy" (Eph. 4:22–24 NLT).

Even though we "should walk in newness of life," as Paul pointed out, it is important to understand that we still have the capacity to sin. The point is that we are no longer under the *jurisdiction* of sin. The previous rights sin had for dominating us and commanding us have been cancelled. We don't have to sin. The tyranny and penalty of sin both in and over the Christian's life has been broken, but sin's potential for expression in his or her life has not been fully removed. Christ died not only to destroy the penalty of past sin, but also to cancel the power of present sin.

Inner Turmoil

Even so, our human weaknesses and instincts make us capable of giving in to the devil's temptations, especially when we live apart from the Holy Spirit's power and God's Word.

> Sin is crouching at our doors too. For some of us, it has already crossed the threshold.

A man from India who wanted to illustrate his new and old natures compared them to two dogs that constantly scrap and fight against one another. He said, "My new nature and old nature are like two dogs that are constantly fighting, but I decide which dog will win."

"How do you decide?" someone asked.

"The one I want to win," he said, "I feed the most."

We have a new nature and an old nature that are constantly battling. Which one will win? You decide by the one you feed the most. By not building up the new nature and neglecting the things of the Spirit, the potential for sin will become stronger and easier every passing day.

Doing Our Part

Paul said, "Likewise you also, reckon yourselves to be dead indeed to sin, but alive to God in Christ Jesus our Lord" (v. 11). God has opened the prison door, but we must walk through it. There are certain things that only God can do, and certain things that only we can do. Only God can justify. Only God can forgive.

But on the other hand, only we can repent. And only we can appropriate and count these things as true in our lives—and start possessing our spiritual possessions.

Sin is a horrible master, and it finds a willing servant in the human body. The human body itself is neutral; it can be controlled either by sin or by God. But the old nature gives sin a beachhead from which it can attack and then control. Paul, lamenting this problem, said, "I know that nothing good lives in me, that is, in my sinful nature. For I have the desire to do what is good, but I cannot carry it out" (Rom. 7:18 NIV).

But an important truth emerges in Romans 6: "Knowing this, that our old man was crucified with Him, that the body of sin might be done away with, that we should no longer be slaves of sin" (v. 6). The "old man," basically, self, was crucified with Christ so that the body need not be controlled by sin. The phrase "done away with" does not mean "annihilated." It means "rendered inactive," "made of no effect," or simply "put out of business."

Sin wants to be our master. God could see this sinful bent in Cain before he killed Abel: "So the Lord said to Cain, 'Why are you angry? And why has your countenance fallen? If you do well, will you not be accepted? And if you do not do well, sin lies at the door. And its desire is for you, but you should rule over it' " (Gen. 4:6–7). The phrase "sin lies at the door" could be literally translated, "sin is crouching at your door." Clearly Cain had not been doing well up to this point. God gave Cain a warning. In Cain's refusal to come to God on His terms, he was flirting with disaster. The cause of his anger was sin, and sin was about to master him.

> We must understand that we are
> not remodeled sinners, but remade saints.

Sin is crouching at our doors too. For some of us, it has already crossed the threshold. So what can we do? How can we protect ourselves from the power of the devil and his demon forces?

We must first realize that we cannot do it ourselves. Jesus told the story of a man who had been possessed by a demon, but the demon was driven out. So the demon went and found seven other more wicked demons, and they all returned and possessed the man. Jesus said, "The last state of that man is worse than the first" (Matt. 12:45). The only defense against sin crouching at our door is Jesus Christ. When the devil knocks at your door, it is a good idea to say, "Lord, would you mind getting that?"

Know, Reckon, Yield

Jesus said to the man who was sick for thirty-eight years, "Do you want to be made well?" (John 5:6). Many people do not. There is God's part in all of this and then there is ours. The question is do we really want to be free from sin? And if so, what should we do?

Three words from Romans 6 put it all together for us: know, reckon, and yield. "Know" centers in the mind. "Reckon" focuses on the heart. And "yield" touches on the will.

First, we must *know*. This deals primarily with the mind. Paul began, "Likewise you also … " (v. 11). These three words are crucial to Paul's explanation, referring back to the truths he had just given in verses 1–10. Paul laid the groundwork, showing that we are no longer under the jurisdiction of sin. It no longer has a rightful claim over our lives as children of God.

> Reckoning is not claiming a promise,
> but acting on a fact.

For us as believers to live out the fullness of our new lives in Jesus Christ, for us to truly live as the new creations that we are, we must *know* and believe that we are not what we used to be. We must understand that we are not remodeled sinners, but remade saints. We must understand that despite our present conflict with sin, we are no longer under sin's tyranny and control. This is clearly something the devil doesn't want us to know.

Second, we must *reckon*. This deals primarily with the heart. "Likewise you also, reckon yourselves to be dead indeed to sin, but alive to God in Christ Jesus our Lord" (v. 11). In some parts of our nation, especially many Southern states, "reckon" means "to think" or "to guess." But the biblical use of the word is different altogether. And it is very important for us to understand. It means "count," "impute," "take into account, to calculate," and "to put to one's account and count as true." Paul was not saying that as believers, we need to feel as though we are dead to sin or even that we need to understand it fully. Rather, he was saying that we need to act upon God's Word and count it as true for ourselves.

> Our victory is not in our deadness to sin alone, but also in our aliveness to God.

Reckoning is not acting *as if it were* so; it is acting *because it is* so. Reckoning is not claiming a promise, but acting on a fact. God does not command us to be dead to sin; He tells us we are dead to sin and alive to God—and then commands us to act on it. Even if we do not act on it, the facts are still true. Being dead to sin is only half the story. If it were all the story, then it only would be half enough. Our victory is not in our deadness to sin alone, but also in our aliveness to God. The death to sin is negative, while life in God is positive. The one removes penalty, while the other gives power.

Third, we must *yield*. This deals primarily with the will. "And do not present your members as instruments of unrighteousness to sin, but present yourselves to God as being alive from the dead, and your members as instruments of righteousness to God" (v. 13). The word "present" could also be translated "yield," which means to "place at one's disposal, to offer as a sacrifice." The same word is used again in Romans 12:1, where we are told to "present [our] bodies a living sacrifice. ... " This is an act of the will, based on our knowledge of what Christ has done for us. It is an intelligent action—not an impulsive decision of the moment, based on mere emotional stirring.

It is also important to notice the verb tenses in verse 11. One translation of this verse reads,

> Do not continue offering or yielding your bodily members [and faculties] to sin as instruments (tools) of wickedness. But offer and yield yourselves to God as though you have been raised from the dead to [perpetual] life, and your bodily members [and faculties] to God, presenting them as implements of righteousness. (AMP)

What Will It Be?

Sin has no power to control a believer unless the believer chooses to obey its lusts.

It is also important to note that there is both a positive and negative aspect to the phrase "do not present." We are not to present our members, or "give in," to these sins.

The Bible tells of people who permitted God to take and use their bodies for the fulfilling of His purposes. God used the rod in Moses' hand and conquered Egypt. He used the sling in David's hand to defeat the Philistines. He used the mouths and tongues of the prophets. Paul's dedicated feet carried him from city to city as he proclaimed the gospel. The apostle John's eyes saw visions of the future, his ears heard God's message, and his fingers wrote it all down in a book that we can read today.

But the Bible also tells of people who did just the opposite, people who used the members of their bodies for sinful purposes. David's eyes looked upon his neighbor's wife, his mind plotted a wicked scheme, and his hand signed a cowardly order for the woman's husband to be killed. Judas Iscariot's feet led the way for Jesus' captors, and his lips delivered the kiss that betrayed Him. The hands of the religious leaders picked up stones to murder Stephen, the first martyr of the church.

These were the choices they made. And each and every day, we make a choice regarding whom or what we are going to yield to. When you get up tomorrow, you can occupy your mind with the things of God or fill it with useless clutter—or worse, with sinful things.

You can spend your time using your lips to glorify and honor God and build up people, or you can engage in slander, gossip, or other things that dishonor the Lord. There are so many choices that you will make.

God has given you the resources for the life that He wants you to live. Now is the time for you to know what they are, to count them as true in your own life, and then to yield all of yourself to Him.

Justification is a legal act of God, declaring the sinner guiltless before God. It is a complete acquittal. When God justifies us, He does so by placing the righteousness of Christ into our account.

Sanctification means being "set apart." That is, set apart to be used by God and to become more like Christ.

5 What's Your Story?

I love a good story, especially a true story about a real person. When I go on vacation and take along books to read, I generally don't choose fiction. I prefer biographies. I am always interested in all types of biographies of different people from different walks of life. And I am as interested in their failures as in their successes. I want to know what makes them tick and what they went through in their lives. The stories of people have always interested me.

A testimony is a bridge–builder.

Everyone likes to hear a good story, especially a true story. And when it comes to sharing your faith, one of the most effective tools in your evangelistic toolbox is your personal testimony. A testimony is a bridge-builder. It is a way to connect with your listener so he or she can see how you came to be who you are and why you believe what you believe. And it can help your listener see how he or she can come to faith as well. It is also a great way to engage a person.

Another great thing about sharing your testimony is that you can inadvertently preach the gospel. Instead of abruptly saying, "You are a sinner. You need to repent," you can share the gospel indirectly. You can say something like, "You know, before I was a Christian, my life was going nowhere. There was an emptiness, and I wondered what was wrong, what was missing. One day, I went to a church service and heard the pastor say that we are all separated from God because of our sin. But because God loved us, He sent His own Son to die in our place and bridge the gap between Him and us." Then, when you're finished, you can say something like, "Let me ask you, what do you think about that? Have you ever heard that before?" It is a way to share the gospel while you are telling your own story.

So what's your story? Everyone has one. Everyone has a testimony—and every testimony is valid. Granted, some are more dramatic than others. We have heard the stories of individuals who have been through horrific tragedies and have survived to tell their stories. Then there might be someone who was a gang member, a drug user, an alcoholic, or served time in prison, and his or her testimony is a great before-and-after story. But then there are those with less-than-dramatic stories, such as the relatively moral, honest, hardworking person, who was actually quite successful, but realized his or her need for Jesus as well.

The love of God knows no racial, economic, or even sinful boundaries.

When you really get down to it, everyone's testimony is essentially the same: We all were lost. We all were separated from God. We all were guilty and lonely and afraid to die, and we all were on our way to hell. And Jesus Christ, in His grace, intervened in our lives and transformed us. That is your story and mine—and it is worth telling.

So far, we have learned that the words of the Great Commission were addressed to every follower of Jesus Christ—not just to pastors, teachers, evangelists, or missionaries, but to any person anywhere who names the name of Christ. They are a command from our Lord to go and share the gospel. We have looked at the who, where, why, and what of evangelism. And we have learned what it means to be justified and sanctified.

Now let's look at a classic example of the power of a changed life. There is no better example of how to do evangelism than Jesus Christ himself. He was the Master Communicator, the Master Evangelist. That is beautifully illustrated in the story of His conversation with the woman at the well. We find it in John 4:

> He left Judea and departed again to Galilee. But He needed to go through Samaria. So He came to a city of Samaria which is called Sychar, near the plot of ground that Jacob gave to his son Joseph.

Now Jacob's well was there. Jesus therefore, being wearied from His journey, sat thus by the well. It was about the sixth hour. A woman of Samaria came to draw water. Jesus said to her, "Give Me a drink." (vv. 3–7)

We want to invade our world with the gospel.

Verse 4 tells us, "He needed to go through Samaria." A little historical background will help us to understand some important things here. No orthodox Jew would ever go to Galilee through Samaria. Yet going through Samaria was a shortcut. It would shave a lot of time off the journey. Even so, the reason most Jews would not go through Samaria was because of deep-seated bigotry and prejudice. Samaritans hated Jews. Jews hated Samaritans. Yet Jesus, a Jew and a rabbi, "needed to go through Samaria," the Bible says. But why? Because in Samaria, there was a burned-out, empty, searching, lonely woman who had an appointment with God, unbeknownst to her. She had expressed her sin through rampant immorality, among other things, bouncing from marriage to marriage. Yet Jesus Christ took time for her. In fact, quite a bit of time.

This serves as a reminder that the love of God knows no racial, economic, or even sinful boundaries.

Go Where People Are

The first thing we learn from Jesus' example is that we have to go to where people are. So often Christians will try to isolate themselves from unbelievers. Their goal is to get through a day without any contact with people who aren't yet believers. But as I've said before, God has not called us to isolate; He has called us to infiltrate. That is our mission field. God wants us to reach out to that grumpy neighbor, to that inquisitive coworker always peppering us with questions, and to all those other people we are around in our day-to-day living. Jesus did not say that the whole world should go to church. But He did say that the church should go to the whole world. We want to invade our world with the gospel.

That is one of the one of the reasons we try to do everything we can to reach people in unexpected ways through Harvest Ministries. In addition to our church services and Harvest Crusades, we reach people through the Internet, television, radio, and even podcasts. People are searching. So we need to go where people are.

Use Tact

The second thing we learn is that we need to use tact. Tact has been defined as the intuitive knowledge of saying the right thing at the right time. Jesus, the Master Evangelist, understood this. I have seen how believers sometimes will approach unbelievers with really strange verbiage. They will say something along the lines of, "Hey, you sinner! Heathen Philistine! Come here for a second! Did you know that you are going to hell?" Afterward they will say, "Man, some people are just offended by the gospel!"

> Tact has been defined as the intuitive knowledge of saying the right thing at the right time.

It's true that many times people are offended by the gospel. There is indeed an offense in it. But a lot of times people are offended because Christians are simply weird, unnecessarily offensive, and don't know how to use tact. We believers need to try to bring a little winsomeness to the conversation and tactfully try to engage our listener. We need to try to build a bridge to the person we are speaking with, such as finding something we might have in common. Arrest their attention. The idea is not to win the argument; it's to win the soul. You might start a conversation, have a lot of great information to give them, and then blast them with your argument to the point they don't ever want to ever talk to a Christian again. That accomplishes nothing. What we want to do instead is try to win them over. After all, if you can argue people into the kingdom of God, then they can be argued out as well. As the rock band, Three Dog Night, used to sing, "Try a little tenderness."

It reminds me of the barber who went to church one Sunday, where the pastor told the congregation that they needed to go and preach the gospel. The barber decided that on Monday morning, he would share the gospel with the first person who sat in his chair. He ran a traditional type of barber shop, where he used a straightedge razor for shaving. So sure enough, on Monday morning, a man walked into his shop and sat down in his chair. As the barber picked up his razor and began to vigorously sharpen it, he turned to the man and said, "Friend, are you ready to meet God?" The customer ran out, apron and all. You see, that barber needed to use a little tact. And we need to do the same.

> The idea is not to win the argument;
> it's to win the soul.

Notice how Jesus tactfully and gracefully engaged the Samaritan woman: "Whoever drinks of this water will thirst again, but whoever drinks of the water that I shall give him will never thirst. But the water that I shall give him will become in him a fountain of water springing up into everlasting life" (vv. 13–14). Jesus was using the well and its water as a metaphor for her life. The reason she came to the well at the hottest part of the day was because she was a social outcast. None of the other women would have anything to do with her, because she had been married and divorced five times and was presently living with a man. She was thought of as, and was indeed, a very immoral woman. So Jesus used a metaphor in which He was essentially saying, "I understand what you are doing. You are searching. You are trying to fill a void in your life with men and with sex, and it hasn't worked. And just as you can come to this well of water and not be satisfied, you can come to this well of relationships and the well of pleasure and drink again and again, and you will never be satisfied. But if you drink from the water that I offer, you will never thirst again."

So how did the woman respond? She flippantly shot back, "Sir, give me this water, that I may not thirst, nor come here to draw" (v. 15).

Adapt to the Situation

This brings us to the third thing we see in Jesus' example as Master Evangelist: we must adapt to the situation.

This woman was accustomed to men being harsh with her. Here was this Jewish man engaging her, a Samaritan woman. She probably was bracing herself for the insult, for the put-down. But there was no put-down here with Jesus. It must have been hard for her to let her wall down. It must have been hard for her not to be so cynical. She had been chewed up and spit out by life, used and abused by men, and here was this man talking to her about living water. When she came back at Him with an edge of sarcasm, He identified the fact that she had been living in sin. He put His finger on that dark spot in her life: "You have well said, 'I have no husband,' for you have had five husbands, and the one whom you now have is not your husband; in that you spoke truly" (vv. 17–18).

> If you can argue people into the kingdom of God, then they can be argued out as well.

As I pointed out earlier, people cannot fully appreciate the good news until they first know the bad news. When you are talking to someone about the Lord, he or she might ask whether it's necessary to give up a certain lifestyle. Sometimes Christians are afraid to deal with that. But it is best to be honest and say, "Absolutely you need to turn from that lifestyle, because it is a sin." That might offend them, but it is the truth. Do it lovingly and do it with grace, but don't back off.

When that rich young ruler came to Jesus and said, "Good Teacher, what shall I do to inherit eternal life?" Jesus said, "You still lack one thing. Sell all that you have and distribute to the poor, and you will have treasure in heaven; and come, follow Me" (Luke 18:18). He never said that in particular to any other person. But He told that man to make a sacrifice to follow Him.

As Jesus engaged this woman in dialogue, she was getting uncomfortable. He had turned a laser beam on her sin. So she tried to get Him off the subject: "Our fathers worshiped on this mountain, and you Jews say that in Jerusalem is the place where one ought to worship" (v. 20).

There is a lot of power in the simplicity of a changed life.

There was an ongoing debate between the Jews and the Samaritans about where God was to be worshiped. The Jews believed that He was to be worshiped in Jerusalem, where the temple, priests, and sacrificial system were. It was God's order that He had established. But the Samaritans had their own temple and their own views. Jesus could have really jumped on this issue, because it was a hotly debated topic of that day. But He answered her question very succinctly, pointing out what was right, and then brought it back to the big issue: "God is Spirit, and those who worship Him must worship in spirit and truth" (v. 24).

People will want to send you off on a rabbit trail when you're sharing the gospel. When you start to get personal, when you start talking to them about their need for God, they will come back with comments like, "Well, wait. If God is so good, then why does He allow suffering? And what about people who have never heard about Jesus Christ? What will God do with them?" As you are answering one question, they are moving on to another. That is a diversionary tactic. (In Chapter 7, I will talk more about difficult questions and will try to give you some answers to the questions unbelievers often ask.) When this happens, I try to answer the question to the best of my ability, and then bring it back to the core issue, which is the person's need for Christ.

That is exactly what Jesus did with the Samaritan woman. He brought her back to what really mattered, what was really essential. As a result, her initial cynicism gave way to curiosity. She was starting to believe: " 'I know that Messiah is coming' (who is called Christ). 'When He comes, He will tell us all things.' Jesus said to her, 'I who speak to you am He' " (vv. 25–26).

Tell Your Story

This brings us to the fourth thing we need to remember when we're sharing the gospel: telling our story is a powerful bridge for the gospel message. The Samaritan woman, minutes old in the faith, immediately went out and began to tell others:

> The woman then left her waterpot, went her way into the city, and said to the men, "Come, see a Man who told me all things that I ever did. Could this be the Christ?" Then they went out of the city and came to Him. (vv. 28–30)

There is a lot of power in the simplicity of a changed life. Her testimony was so powerful that people believed as a result. We read that "many of the Samaritans of that city believed in Him because of the word of the woman who testified, 'He told me all that I ever did' " (v. 39). It was the power of a changed life.

That is why it is so important to share the before and after of what God has done in your life. You may have such an amazing story that others find it difficult to believe you are the same person, because your life has been so transformed by Jesus Christ. Sharing about that transformation can really speak to someone in a special way.

I find it interesting how often the apostle Paul, a brilliant orator, a great communicator, and a wonderful intellect, would use his testimony to speak to people. We see in Acts 24 that when he spoke before the Roman governor, he began with his story of how he came to faith. Then he went to the essential core message of the gospel.

So what is the best way to tell your story? What should you include? What should you *not* include?

Don't Glorify or Exaggerate Your Past

First, don't glorify or exaggerate your past. Accuracy is important. So is truthfulness. I bring this up because some Christians' testimonies change with the passing of time, becoming a little more dramatic than they used to be. Be totally honest and tell the truth.

Another problem is making your past sound more appealing than your present. I have heard believers get up and share their testimonies about all the things they once did, and as they are talking about the old days, they make them sound better than the new days! It makes me wonder if they really understand what it means to be a Christian. Paul, in speaking of his past, said,

> I once thought these things were valuable, but now I consider them worthless because of what Christ has done. Yes, everything else is worthless when compared with the infinite value of knowing Christ Jesus my Lord. For his sake I have discarded everything else, counting it all as garbage, so that I could gain Christ. (Phil. 3:7–8 NLT)

The word "garbage" can also be translated as "dung," and "dung" means "dung." Paul was making a point. What word could be more offensive than that? When I walk my dog, I certainly don't enjoy cleaning up after him. The first thing I want to do is find the nearest trash receptacle. I don't save what my dog left behind, and I certainly don't brag about it to other people. I see it for what it is: excrement, refuse.

The seeds you plant today may break ground tomorrow.

If you see your life before Christ as a wonderful thing, then you are not seeing it as it really was. Whatever you were doing, you were headed for a certain judgment, and God, in His grace, invaded your world and brought you to faith. When you tell your story, instead of glorifying your past, glorify the Lord and talk about what He has done for you.

Remember, It's about Him

Second, when you tell your story, remember that it's not about you. It's about Him. Don't dwell too long on your story, because it is a bridge— a bridge to get to the big story of Jesus. Make a beeline to the cross.

That is the part of the story you want to get to: His love for humanity, His death, His resurrection from the dead, and how He can transform peoples' lives.

Be Patient

We must be patient in the work of sharing the gospel. I cannot emphasize enough that conversion is the work of God and God alone. He is looking for laborers in the field, and every one of us has an important part to play. Sometimes it is just planting a seed. At other times, it is watering a seed that someone else has planted. And sometimes, by God's grace, it is reaping what others have planted and watered. Following this line of thinking, Paul said,

> I planted, Apollos watered, but God gave the increase. So then neither he who plants is anything, nor he who waters, but God who gives the increase. Now he who plants and he who waters are one, and each one will receive his own reward according to his own labor. (1 Cor. 3:6–8)

Just be faithful in getting that seed started. Sometimes it is sharing the entire gospel. At other times, it is telling a little of your story. Sometimes it is just saying to an unbeliever who is hurting, "I will remember to pray for you." Sometimes it is just being a good example. My point is that you are planting little seeds.

Then again, you might be watering seeds that others have planted. As you look back on your own conversion, you probably can recall the events that led to it. There were certain things that began to soften your heart, things that touched you and made you more open and receptive to the gospel. Therefore, those seeds that are being planted today in the lives of unbelievers are so important.

Maybe you get a little discouraged because you've been doing a lot of planting, but you haven't seen any results. A farmer needs to be patient. Ecclesiastes 3:11 says, "Yet God has made everything beautiful for its own time. He has planted eternity in the human heart, but even so, people cannot see the whole scope of God's work from beginning to end" (Eccl. 3:11 NLT).

We must be patient in planting seeds and in sharing the gospel and not give up. As Paul wrote to Timothy, "A servant of the Lord must not quarrel but must be kind to everyone, be able to teach, and be patient with difficult people" (2 Tim. 2:24 NLT).

The seeds you plant today may break ground tomorrow. That bit of truth you shared with someone might be like a time bomb that detonates later, because God says that His Word will not return void (see Isa. 55:11). You see, the harvest is not at the end of a service; it is at the end of the age. So we need to keep praying and believing that God will use His Word.

I have done funeral services for Christians who had been praying for someone their entire lives, only to have that person come to Christ at their funeral. We don't know when the seeds we have planted are going to break ground.

> The harvest is not at the end of
> a service; it is at the end of the age.

Many times we are tempted to think we haven't made a difference for the kingdom, like the missionary named George Smith, who thought his entire ministry was a failure. He had been in Africa only a short time when he was driven from the country. He left behind a Bible and one convert, a poor woman. Not long after that, George Smith died on his knees, praying for Africa.

A number of years later, a group of men stumbled into the place in Africa where George Smith had ministered. They found the woman, who testified to them of her faith in Christ. Then she led them to Christ. Afterward, those men went out and reached others. And the ones they reached also reached others. One hundred years later when a missions organization did a study on the ministry of George Smith, they found more than 15,000 converts who could be directly traced to the one woman he led to Christ so many years earlier.

Like George Smith, maybe you will reach only one person in your entire life. But what if that person becomes another Billy Graham? Maybe you will reach only a handful of people and never see the fruit of it in your lifetime. It may not be until years after you have gone. But God will be faithful with His Word.

We are told in Galatians 6:9, "And let us not grow weary while doing good, for in due season we shall reap if we do not lose heart." So just be faithful. Keep planting those seeds. Keep praying for those who don't know Christ. Keep looking for ways to build bridges to unbelievers. Keep sharing your story of what God has done for you.

Three Keys to Sharing Your Story [5]

1. *Your life before Christ.* Don't glorify your past, but mention how you were before Christ. Share how you never felt that you could become the person you ought to be.

2. *Your life changed by Christ.* Summarize how you came into a relationship with Christ, and be sure to mention the key elements of the gospel.

3. *Your new life in Christ.* Talk about how your life is noticeably different now that you are in Christ. Put into your own words the following benefits of being in Christ: peace (see Rom. 5:1), a purpose for living (see Jer. 29:11), and the assurance that you're going to heaven (see John 3:36).

6 Sharing the Gospel Effectively

Is there a right and wrong way to share the gospel of Jesus Christ? Are there certain essentials that need to be in our presentation so that the gospel truly will be the gospel? Is there a way to be more effective in doing this? The answer to all those questions is a resounding yes!

It has been said there are two reasons people don't go to church:

1. They don't know a Christian.
2. They do know a Christian.

Sometimes we are our own worst enemies. We console ourselves with the words of Matthew 5:10, "Blessed are those who are persecuted for righteousness' sake, for theirs is the kingdom of heaven," but as already stated, we are often "persecuted" for being obnoxious, strange, or just plain weird. And far too often, the worst offenders are the ones who should be the greatest example: preachers. I have often wondered where many of the bizarre ministers we see on television come from. And do they talk that way all the time? It is embarrassing. People will look at these self-appointed representatives of the Christian faith and write off all Christians. But if all I knew of Christianity was what I see on some Christian television programs today, I would think Christians were crazy too.

Sometimes we are our own worst enemies.

Many times, unbelievers are not rejecting the gospel as much as they are rejecting the way it is presented. It is not what's inside of the box that they are rejecting, but the wrapping in which it is delivered.

That is not to say there isn't an offense in the message of the gospel, because indeed there can be. Yet at the same time, let's make sure it is the gospel they are offended by instead of some strange thing that an alleged follower of Christ says or does.

In Acts 14, we find the record of Paul's first missionary journey. Paul was called by God to preach the gospel, and he was an effective communicator of it. Here we see what God can do in the life of a believer who is available to Him. We also see what the devil will attempt to do to the man or woman who steps out from the crowd to proclaim the gospel.

Anticipating Attacks

The devil will always oppose the person whom God is using. When Christians, motivated by love for lost people, seek to reach out and invite them to heaven, the devil, motivated by hate, seeks to reach out and pull them down to hell. When the people of God say, "Let us rise up and build," the devil and his demons say, "Let us rise up and oppose." Don't let that terrify you, but let it educate you. Jesus said we are His church, and "the gates of Hades shall not prevail against it" (Matt. 16:18).

> Let's make sure it is the
> gospel they are offended by.

We also see in Acts 14 two modes of attack often used by the enemy, designed to stop the person whom God is using:

1. *Outward attack:* "But the unbelieving Jews stirred up the Gentiles and poisoned their minds against the brethren" (v. 2); "Then Jews from Antioch and Iconium came there; and having persuaded the multitudes, they stoned Paul and dragged him out of the city, supposing him to be dead" (v. 19). Paul's outward attacks came in the form of slander, the threat of losing his life, and actual physical harm.

2. *Inward (or sneak) attack:* "Now when the people saw what Paul had done, they raised their voices, saying in the Lycaonian language, 'The gods have come down to us in the likeness of men!' " (v. 11). Paul's inward attack came in the form of the worship of the people. Popularity is often more deadly than persecution. One begins to believe his or her own press and becomes inflated with pride.

At first when God begins to use you, the devil whispers in your ear, "You're not worthy to be used by God," or "You'll fail. No one will listen to you. ... " That is when you decide to ignore him, remem-bering that "God has chosen the foolish things of the world to put to shame the wise" (1 Cor. 1:27) and "The eyes of the Lord run to and fro throughout the whole earth, to show Himself strong on behalf of those whose heart is loyal to Him" (2 Chron. 16:9).

So the devil changes his tactic. He whispers, "You're so wonderful! No one prays like you do. You're so powerful when you speak!" This tactic is much easier to succumb to, because many times you don't even realize that it's happening. Satan recognizes the biblical prin-ciple that pride goes before a fall (see Prov. 16:18). This was Samson's problem. He thought he could handle things. We think his main sin was immorality, but it primarily was the root sin of pride that made him think he could do whatever he wanted with impunity. But his sin found him out.

It brings to mind a news story I read about a teenager in Mil-waukee who was suspected of stealing a wireless microphone from a local church. He apparently forgot to check to see whether it was turned on. People in church on a Saturday night were shocked to hear obscenities streaming through the sanctuary speakers. Some people from the church investigated and found the fourteen-year-old shout-ing into the microphone. They captured him after a chase that lasted several blocks. Sin makes you do stupid things.

Peter was also brought down by the devil's tactic of pride. We know that he denied the Lord three times. But the pride that pre-ceded his denial was the root sin. In the Upper Room, he had said to Jesus, "Even if all are made to stumble because of You, I will never be made to stumble" (Matt. 26:33).

The best way we can pray for the person God is using, as well as for ourselves, is to ask God to help us remain humble and usable.

How easily Paul could have compromised in this area and rationalized that he would first draw the people to himself and then he would tell them about Jesus. But once that path is taken, so many compromises will have been made that no one will want to listen once we get there.

The Catfish in Your Tank

Paul, after his difficulties, laid it out plainly for the believers: "We must through many tribulations enter the kingdom of God" (v. 22). Paul later wrote to Timothy, "Yes, and all who desire to live godly in Christ Jesus will suffer persecution" (2 Tim. 3:12).

> ## Sin makes you do stupid things.

In a lot of ways, you could say we are like the cod that were shipped from the East Coast to the West Coast. By the time the fish arrived in the west, it was spoiled. The supplier tried freezing the fish, only to have it arrive mushy to the taste. They tried shipping the fish live, but they arrived dead. So they tried sending them live once again, but with one difference: they included catfish in the tanks. Catfish are the mortal enemies of cod, so the cod arrived alive and well, having spent their trip eluding the catfish. People who ate the fish said it was the best they had ever tasted.

In the same way, God may put a catfish in your tank, so to speak, to keep you alive and well spiritually. That is where persecution comes in. Consider what Jesus said about this:

> "If the world hates you, you know that it hated Me before it hated you. If you were of the world, the world would love its own. Yet because you are not of the world, but I chose you out of the world, therefore the world hates you. Remember the word that I said to you, 'A servant is not greater than his master.' If they persecuted Me, they will also persecute you." (John 15:18–20)

Whenever the devil sees a work of God beginning to flourish, he throws up a roadblock. It may be an unexpected delay or even someone among our ranks who opposes it. Judas, after all, was against Mary's pouring her perfume on the feet of Jesus, protesting, "Why was this fragrant oil not sold for three hundred denarii and given to the poor?" (John 12:5). It sounded noble, but the truth of the matter was that Judas was the treasurer, and he was skimming from the money box.

Whenever you attempt to do something to reach an unbeliever with the gospel, you will face clear-cut, satanic opposition.

The Secret of the "So"

Thankfully, Paul never allowed persecution to deter him, but instead was a persistent and effective communicator of the gospel. Acts 14:1 tells us, "Now it happened in Iconium that they went together to the synagogue of the Jews, and *so spoke* that a great multitude both of the Jews and of the Greeks believed" (emphasis mine). The word "so" in this verse arrests our attention and says to all preachers, teachers, and everyone called to declare the gospel that there is a way to "so speak" that people will believe.

It appears from this verse that there is a right way and a wrong way to declare the gospel. Some people, in the way they declare it, make it the bad news instead of the Good News.

> Some people make it the bad news instead of the Good News.

Others want to make the gospel acceptable, so they will water it down and not declare the "whole counsel of God" (see Acts 20:27). It is tempting to conveniently leave out that which is uncomfortable to say. But what would you think of a doctor who would not deliver any bad news? He or she might insist, "I don't want to offend anyone." But if people are given the truth, then they can do something about it. If not, they will die. It is better to make someone uncomfortable temporarily than to send them to death permanently.

Still others will try to make the gospel so eloquent that they will complicate the absolute simplicity of the message. Paul said, "And I, brethren, when I came to you, did not come with excellence of speech or of wisdom declaring to you the testimony of God" (1 Cor. 2:1) and "Christ did not send me to baptize, but to preach the gospel, not with wisdom of words, lest the cross of Christ should be made of no effect" (1 Cor. 1:17).

It is not your objective to impress your listener with your theological depth or intellectual prowess. It is to speak in a way that they can understand and then respond.

The average American did not graduate from college and does not know the difference between evangelist and evangelical. You need to break things down in an understandable way.

Here we discover the secret of the "so"—in other words, the secret of effectively sharing the gospel:

- It will be clear, simple, and focused on the work of Jesus Christ on the cross.
- It will be unapologetically biblical.
- It will be truthful, yet lovingly shared.

Mistaken Identities

It is hard to comprehend how the crowd at Lystra could be so superstitious, but history sheds a great deal of light on it. About fifty years earlier, the poet Ovid had narrated an ancient local legend. The supreme god, Jupiter (Zeus) and his son Mercury (Hermes) once visited the hill country of Phrygia, disguised as mortal men. Traveling incognito, they were turned away one thousand times. Finally they were offered lodging by an elderly peasant couple named Baucis and Philemon, whose tiny cottage was thatched with reeds and straw from the marsh. Later these gods rewarded them, but they destroyed the rest of the homes by flood, because the people would not take them in.

Also, apart from the literary evidence left by Ovid, two inscriptions and a stone altar have been discovered near Lystra, which indicates that Zeus and Hermes were worshiped together locally as patron deities.

So avoiding the temptation to compromise and give in to pride by allowing himself and Barnabas to be worshiped as Zeus and Hermes, Paul seized the opportunity to speak the truth to these pagan-worshiping people.

God the Creator

He began by speaking of the true God who created all things: "Men, why are you doing these things? We also are men with the same nature as you, and preach to you that you should turn from these useless things to the living God, who made the heaven, the earth, the sea, and all things that are in them" (v. 15).

There are those who say they don't believe that God created all things, but that humans evolved from a lower life-form. In most cases, the reason for this so-called belief is not because they have honestly taken the time to study the biblical teaching of creationism or the theory of evolution. Rather, they use it as a convenient hook on which to hang their doubts. C. S. Lewis said that even atheists have their moments of doubt. The theory of evolution flatly contradicts two known laws of science.

> The theory of evolution flatly contradicts two known laws of science.

The first is the universal law of conservation of energy. Evolution teaches that creation is continually being accomplished by nature's evolutionary processes. But the most basic law of science, the law of conservation of energy, states that nothing is now being created or destroyed.

The second law evolution contradicts is thermodynamics. One of the most well-established principles in all of science, it says that the natural tendency is for things to go from a more ordered state to a less ordered state. Evolution involves universal change upward, whereas the real processes of nature involve a universal change downward.

The biblical concept of special creation of all the basic kinds of plants and animals, with provision for ample variation within the kinds, is much more in accord with the actual facts and laws of science than is the speculative philosophy of universal evolutionary development. Thus, evolution is not really a science, but a religious philosophy.

Although an evolutionist, Dr. David Kitts of the University of Oklahoma says, "Despite the bright hope that paleontology provides a means of 'seeing' evolution, it has provided some nasty difficulties for the evolutionist, the most notorious of which is the presence of "gaps" in the fossil record. Evolution requires intermediate forms between species and paleontology does not provide them."[6]

Writing in a May 1973 article for *Science Digest,* noted atheist Isaac Asimov acknowledged, "As far as we know, all changes are in the direction of increasing entropy, of increasing disorder, of increasing randomness, of running down."

God has and is showing himself in this world.

There has been for years the search for life on other planets, in hopes that the evolutionary theory someday will be vindicated by evidence that life has also developed elsewhere in the universe. As yet, despite the space probes, giant telescopes, and even the UFO craze, the idea of extraterrestrial life remains nothing more than science fiction for movies like *E.T., Close Encounters of the Third Kind, Men in Black,* and *Independence Day.* There is not the slightest evidence of biological life, as we understand it, anywhere else in the universe. They thought they had found it with a rock discovery that was allegedly from Mars. The "life" they found on the rock was simply microscopic growth from its contact with Earth. The Bible tells us the real reason people believe these theories:

> For since the creation of the world God's invisible qualities—his eternal power and divine nature—have been clearly seen, being understood from what has been made, so that men are without excuse.

For although they knew God, they neither glorified him as God nor gave thanks to him, but their thinking became futile and their foolish hearts were darkened. Although they claimed to be wise, they became fools. (Rom. 1:20–22 NIV)

God has and is showing himself in this world, but people just don't want to see Him or know Him.

They are not much different from those in the crowd at Lystra. When the people realized Paul and Barnabas were not Zeus and Hermes, they quickly turned on them: "Then Jews from Antioch and Iconium came there; and having persuaded the multitudes, they stoned Paul and dragged him out of the city, supposing him to be dead" (v. 19).

A Glimpse of Heaven

Here we see how fickle a mob can be, just like the multitudes that surrounded Jesus. The same mob that shouted their "hosannas" and waved palm branches to herald Jesus' arrival in Jerusalem were demanding his death just a few days later. And the very same people who had worshiped Paul and Barnabas as gods stoned them at the instigation of troublemaking Jews from Antioch and Iconium.

One wonders whether Paul, as he was being stoned, thought back to young Stephen who suffered the same fate at his command. Whether Paul came close to death or actually died, this is most likely the time when he made the short visit to heaven that he spoke of in 2 Corinthians 12:

I know a man in Christ who fourteen years ago was caught up to the third heaven. Whether it was in the body or out of the body I do not know—God knows. And I know that this man— whether in the body or apart from the body I do not know, but God knows—was caught up to paradise. He heard inexpressible things, things that man is not permitted to tell. (vv. 2–4)

It's worth noting that in contrast to the many near-death experiences people have described, Paul said the things he saw were inexpressible. Some people who claim to have visited heaven go into great detail as to what they saw and heard. They maintain that special messages were given to them by God, which, of course, they are happy to reveal for a price.

I prefer to stay with the biblical accounts that give us brief glimpses of what happens beyond the grave. In fact, all other accounts should be compared to these biblical ones. For Paul, it was not yet time for him to die. God still had work for him to do:

> But after the disciples had gathered around him, he got up and went back into the city. The next day he and Barnabas left for Derbe. They preached the good news in that city and won a large number of disciples. Then they returned to Lystra, Iconium and Antioch, strengthening the disciples and encouraging them to remain true to the faith. (vv. 20–22)

Paul continued preaching the gospel message, undeterred by the tremendous obstacles he encountered. He stands as a great example to us today of what it means to communicate the gospel clearly, intelligently, and uncompromisingly. May we do the same.

The Secret of the "So"

What makes an effective presentation of the gospel?

- It is clear, simple, and focused on the work of Jesus Christ on the cross.
- It is unapologetically biblical.
- It is truthful, yet lovingly shared.

7 Prepared to Share: Five Questions Unbelievers Ask

After experiencing surprising success in my very first, albeit rather awkward, attempt at sharing the gospel as a new Christian, I was feeling quite confident. I wanted to reach even more people. So once again, I went down to the beach, where thousands of people gathered, to find someone to share the gospel with. As I was walking down the street, I ran into an old friend named Gregg. We had gone through elementary, junior high, and high school together. I used to hang around him a lot, and we used drugs together. He looked at me, and I looked at him, and we both started laughing. There was a reason for that.

Christianity is a very logical belief.

Not long after I had given my life to Christ, I went back to my old buddies that I hung out with and told them I wasn't going to become a fanatic. "I have accepted Jesus into my life," I told them, "but there is one thing you are never going to see Greg Laurie do. You are never going to see me walking around with a Bible under my arm. And you are never going to hear me say, "Praise the Lord!" or have some little fish symbol or cross hanging around my neck. I'm going to do this in a modified way. You'll see."

So there I was, walking down the sidewalk of Newport toward Gregg. Under my arm … a Bible. Around my neck (you guessed it) … a fish symbol. And before I could catch myself, I blurted out to my old buddy Gregg, "Praise the Lord!" That's why we both started laughing. The impossible had taken place in mere days.

You would have had to have known me before to appreciate this rapid change. Because of my difficult upbringing with my alcoholic mother, I had become a pretty cynical young man. Always quick with a fast retort or wisecrack, I was not what you would consider a prime candidate for conversion. I had openly laughed at the Christians on my high school campus, and now, here I was one of them! Not only that, but I was trying to reach others with the same message that had changed my life.

There is not a one–size–fits–all approach to evangelism.

As we joked about this I said, "Gregg, this is so funny. Let me tell you something. Jesus Christ has changed my life. I want to tell you about it." Then I began to share what I had learned in church, although it wasn't a lot at the time. I still was only a few weeks old in the faith. Even so, I shared everything that I knew about God with my friend. I noticed he was warming up to it. He was paying attention. He was listening. I thought, *What if he came to the Lord right now? Wouldn't that be great?*

Suddenly a guy came walking up to me and said, "I have a few questions for you, Christian." Apparently he had been eavesdropping on our conversation. Then he proceeded to rattle off four or five questions. I don't even recall what they were. But I do remember that I was dumbfounded. I didn't have a clue.

Then Gregg turned to me and said, "Yeah, Laurie, what about those things?"

"I don't know," I sheepishly admitted. I was devastated. At this point, I realized that I needed to better prepare myself. I began to put into practice the words of 2 Timothy 2:15: "Be diligent to present yourself approved to God, a worker who does not need to be ashamed, rightly dividing the word of truth."

After all these years, I still don't have the answer to every question. But the Bible does. So we need to arm ourselves when we go and share our faith with others.

We are told in 1 Peter 3:15,

> But in your hearts set apart Christ as Lord. Always be prepared
> to give an answer to everyone who asks you to give the reason
> for the hope that you have. But do this with gentleness and
> respect, keeping a clear conscience, so that those who speak
> maliciously against your good behavior in Christ may be
> ashamed of their slander. (NIV)

The word Peter used for "answer" comes from the Greek word
apologia, from which we get our English word "apologetic." This
doesn't mean that we need to learn how to apologize for our faith.
Rather, *apologia* is a legal term used to describe what attorneys do
as they are giving a legal defense in a court of law. We as believers
should be able to give that same kind of defense for the gospel.

Contrary to what some may think, Christianity is a very logical
belief. Isaiah 1:18 says, " 'Come now, and let us reason together,'
says the Lord, 'Though your sins are like scarlet, they shall be
as white as snow; though they are red like crimson, they shall
be as wool.' " Or, as another translation puts it, "Come. Sit down.
Let's argue this out … " (THE MESSAGE).

He often answered a question with a question.

That is not to say there isn't a place for faith, but we don't have to
check our brains at the door when we commit our lives to Christ.
It was when I believed in Jesus and the Bible that the world made
sense to me. Finally I could understand why people did what they
did and how lives could be changed. As C. S. Lewis said, "I believe
in Christianity as I believe that the Sun has risen, not only because
I see it, but because by it I see everything else."[7]

Although *apologia* speaks of giving a legal defense, we need to
remember that we are not the prosecuting attorney, but witnesses.
Remember, our goal is to build a bridge, not burn one.

So in a loving, winsome, graceful, yet bold way, we should seek to engage people:

> A servant of the Lord must not quarrel but must be kind to everyone, be able to teach, and be patient with difficult people. Gently instruct those who oppose the truth. Perhaps God will change those people's hearts, and they will learn the truth. Then they will come to their senses and escape from the devil's trap. For they have been held captive by him to do whatever he wants. (2 Tim. 2:24–26 NLT)

We want to dialogue, not monologue.

We've seen how Jesus masterfully did this as He engaged the Samaritan woman and won her over. She tried to steer Him off course, but He gently brought her back.

Many of us know what it's like to share the gospel with someone, only to be barraged with arguments and questions that are very difficult to answer. Either we will determine to never again confront a person with the gospel, which would be disobedient to what God commanded, or we can seek to find the answers.

The Bible is intended to be a book of redemption.

There are people who have honest questions, and when given an answer, it's as though the stone has been rolled away from their tomb of unbelief. Then there are those who are off to their next question, or the reason they don't come to Christ, before you can even finish answering the question they have just asked. Many times it is not because they want answers. It is because they are trying to deflect what you are saying. We need to know the difference, and then we need to arm ourselves with a working knowledge of the gospel so we can engage the unbeliever.

Let me point out, however, that Jesus never dealt with any two people in exactly the same way. As I have written earlier, the goal is not to win the argument, but the soul. There is not a one-size-fits-all approach to evangelism. Paul said,

God can speak of the future with absolute certainty.

Even though I am a free man with no master, I have become a slave to all people to bring many to Christ. … When I am with those who are weak, I share their weakness, for I want to bring the weak to Christ. Yes, I try to find common ground with everyone, doing everything I can to save some. I do everything to spread the Good News and share in its blessings. (2 Cor. 9:19, 22–23 NLT)

Jesus adapted. His conversation with the Samaritan woman (see John 4) was quite different from his conversation with Nicodemus (see John 3). It is interesting to note how often He asked questions. And He often answered a question with a question. When the rich young ruler came to Jesus and asked, "What good thing shall I do that I may have eternal life?" he could have been a great spokesperson for the cause of Christ. It was one thing to have fishermen, tax collectors, and the like, but a rich, influential man in authority? A man like that could open some doors and perhaps even add some credibility to the ministry—not to mention help underwrite it. But Jesus didn't even give the man the gospel initially. Instead, He asked him a probing question: "Why do you call Me good? No one is good but One, that is, God" (Matt. 19:17). Jesus knew this man wasn't completely sincere. So He was drawing him out and giving him an opportunity to believe.

In the same way, asking questions is a great way to dialogue with people. But remember, we want to dialogue, not monologue. For example, someone might ask, "Do you think Jesus was more than a great moral teacher?"

Instead of immediately answering, try to find common ground. Answer a question with a question: "What makes you think Jesus was a great moral teacher? Have you read His teachings? If so, what do you think is the most important thing He said?"

One-half of the Bible's prophecies have already taken place.

The answer usually will be that they have never read His teachings. This gives you the opportunity to point out some of them.

If someone asks, "What about the person who has never heard the gospel? Will God send them to hell?" you could respond with, "Why do you ask that? Do you believe in hell? Do you think anyone deserves to go there? If not, why? You mentioned the gospel—have you heard it? If so, do you believe it?"

There was the time the religious leaders tried to trap Jesus with a tax issue: "Tell us, therefore, what do You think? Is it lawful to pay taxes to Caesar, or not?" (Matt. 22:17). If Jesus sad it was lawful, the people would turn on Him, because they were overtaxed. If He said it was not lawful, the government would turn on Him, as that would be rebellion.

Our general tendency is to blame God for evil and suffering, and pass all responsibility on to Him.

So instead, Jesus asked for a Roman coin. And again, He answered a question with a question:

> And He said to them, "Whose image and inscription is this?" They said to Him, "Caesar's." And He said to them, "Render therefore to Caesar the things that are Caesar's, and to God the things that are God's." When they had heard these words, they marveled, and left Him and went their way. (Matt. 22:20–22)

Talk about turning a situation around. That is why we must listen carefully and pray for wisdom.

Now let's look at some of the difficult questions unbelievers ask.

1. "How do you know that the Bible is the Word of God? It was written by men, and it's full of contradictions!"

The Bible is the most amazing book ever written. It is literally God's message to you. Technically speaking, it is not one book, but sixty-six, written over a 1,500-year span. Its words were written by more than forty authors from every walk of life, including kings, peasants, philosophers, fishermen, poets, statesmen, and scholars. Yet *all* the authors of the Bible write about one theme: God's redemption of humankind. Each one of these men was inspired by God to write these words. As 2 Peter 1:20–21 says, "Above all, you must understand that no prophecy of Scripture came about by the prophet's own interpretation. For prophecy never had its origin in the will of man, but men spoke from God as they were carried along by the Holy Spirit" (NIV).

So how can we know the Bible is true?

It Gives Us the Experience It Claims It Will

First, I know it is true because it gives me the experience it claims it will give me. That is not the only reason I believe it (and perhaps not the most convincing reason to the skeptic), but it certainly helped me to believe.

For example, the Bible says that God will forgive my sins (see 1 John 1:9). One day I chose to believe that. I accepted God's forgiveness, and suddenly my sense of guilt and the heavy burden I had been carrying were taken away.

The Bible also says that if I come to Christ, then I will become a different person (see 2 Cor. 5:17). I came to Christ, and that has happened to me. Of course, I am still a work in progress, but that change has taken place.

The Bible says that God will give me His peace and joy if I trust Christ (see Gal. 5:22). That, too, has happened.

The Bible says that God will answer my prayers—if I pray properly (see 1 John 5:14). I did that, and my prayers have been answered.

Confirmed by Science

The second reason I know the Bible is true is because it is confirmed by science. You may think the Bible and science contradict each other. But that is not necessarily true. Many people have scoffed at the Bible, believing the assertions that it is unscientific.

Yet it was the Bible that first said the number of the stars is beyond counting. God said to Abraham, "I will multiply your descendants as the stars of the heaven and as the sand which is on the seashore ... " (Gen. 22:17). And Isaiah tells us that God "stretched forth the heavens" (KJV). Still, to your average observer looking into the sky—even with the latest telescope—the visible stars do not look uncountable. They are a vast number, but they do not seem impossible to count. However, the Bible flatly states that the number of the stars can be compared, literally, to the number of grains of sand on the seashore. Modern science has now established this as truth. We cannot possibly begin to assess the number of the stars.

It was the Bible that said, "By faith we understand that the universe was formed at God's command, so that what is seen was not made out of what was visible" (Heb. 11:3 NIV). This statement predates, by many centuries, the discoveries of modern science, which finally recognized that all matter is made up of invisible energy (protons, neutrons, and electrons).

I don't believe in the Bible because science is true. Rather, I believe in the science that the Bible proves is true. Having said that, let me point out something about the Bible that is very important for us to know. It is not the intention of the Bible to be a textbook on science, per se. If it were, it would be much thicker than it is and much less comprehensible. When it addresses scientific or historical fact, it is always accurate. The Bible is intended to be a book of redemption. It tells us how to know God and how to live in this troubled and confused human race. It is the only book that speaks with authority in this realm.

It Is Confirmed by Archaeology

The third reason I believe the Bible is true is because it is confirmed by archaeology. Over the years, countless critics have challenged the teachings of the Bible. But recent archaeological findings have confirmed Scripture's teaching time and time again.

> The point we must keep in mind is that people—not God—are responsible for sin.

Critics have doubted the Bible because of what it said about crucifixion, contending that crucifixion did not take place historically, as Scripture suggests. Such a criticism strikes at the very heart of our faith, as so much is said specifically about the crucifixion of Jesus. But this criticism was silenced in 1968 when the remains of a man crucified in his mid-thirties were discovered north of Jerusalem, with a seven-inch iron nail still embedded in his heel. The state of the bones indicated that the condemned man's arms were outstretched and that his feet had been place sideways, with the nail driven first through a small block of wood and then through both heels into the cross. Once again, the Bible presented the information before the so-called experts had it.

Critics have doubted the Bible over the years, because they could find no historical record of a Roman governor named Pontius Pilate. But in 1961, an inscription found at Caesarea Maritima confirmed that Pontius Pilate was the Roman Governor in Judea at the time of Jesus' crucifixion.

Critics doubted the authority of Scripture because no record of a high priest named Caiaphas existed. But in 1990, the tomb of the high priest Caiaphas was discovered. Jewish historian Dr. Nelson Gleuck has said, "It may be stated categorically that no archaeological discovery has ever controverted a biblical reference. Scores of archaeological findings have been made that confirm in clear outline or in exact detail historical statements in the Bible."[8]

It Is the One Book that
Dares to Predict the Future

The fourth reason I believe the Bible is true is because it is the one book that dares to predict the future. I am not talking about so-called psychics or tabloid predictions. I am talking about very specific prophecies that have been fulfilled. No other world religions have books that do this. Why? If they were to attempt it, it would be evident that they are not inspired by God, which the Bible is.

God can speak of the future with absolute certainty, because He knows it as well as we know the past (even better, because we often forget what actually happened). The basic test of the true God, the true faith, the true prophet, and the true belief lies in this: Can they predict the future? The Bible is one book that does—not once or twice, but hundreds of times. The conflict in the Middle East has been predicted in the Bible, which says that the Jews would regather in their land, would be surrounded by enemies, and that the final world conflict would revolve around the little city of Jerusalem.

One-half of the Bible's prophecies have already taken place. Therefore, if one-half of them have happened as God said they would, should I have any reason to doubt that the remaining ones will happen exactly as God has said? This helps us to see that when God says something will happen, you can take it to the bank.

> It is a great comfort for me to know
> that God loves me enough to correct me.

A scientist figured out the odds of just eight prophecies being fulfilled by coincidence.

The chance that Jesus would be born in Bethlehem? One in 280,000.

The chance that He would have a forerunner announcing His coming? One in 1,000.

The chance that He would be betrayed for thirty pieces of silver? One in 10,000.

The chance that He would have His hands wounded?
One in 10,000.

The chance that He would ride into Jerusalem on a donkey?
One in 1,000.

And if you put them all together, the chance that these things happened coincidentally? One in 10^{27}.

If you were to cover the entire state of Texas with silver dollars two feet thick, mark one, blindfold someone, and then have that person walk across the state and randomly reach down and pick up the one that was marked, that is the chance that Jesus could have fulfilled even eight prophecies by coincidence.

Sincerity is never enough.
We must have a set of absolutes to live by.

The fact is that Jesus fulfilled many, many prophecies. That is not to mention the prophecies fulfilled in other portions of Scripture. So you can see why this Book has been under attack over the years. Ultimately, the issue of believing the Bible comes down to faith.

2. How could a God of love allow suffering? Why is there sickness, even death? Why are babies born with disabilities? Why did He allow tragedies like the Holocaust and 9/11?

When Jesus and the disciples encountered a man who had been blind from birth, the disciples asked Him, "Rabbi, who sinned, this man or his parents, that he was born blind?" (John 9:2). Their question reminds us of the often-asked question of why God allows suffering.

There are many who have turned against God because of a tragedy early in life. Maybe you feel as though you were dealt a harsh hand in the game of life. Perhaps your parents divorced, a loved one died unexpectedly, you have a disability (or know someone who does), and you ask, "Why?"

Our human intellects and notions of fairness reject the apparent contradiction between a loving God and a world of pain. In the classic statement of the problem, either God is all-powerful, but not all good. Therefore, He doesn't stop evil. Or, He is all good but not all-powerful. Therefore, He can't stop evil. Our general tendency is to blame God for evil and suffering, and pass all responsibility on to Him.

God doesn't send anyone to hell; we send ourselves there.

The question that was being asked on the day Jesus met the blind man was can our physical suffering on Earth be the result of sin? Jesus' answer was, "Neither this man nor his parents sinned ... " (v. 3). Meaning, there was no correlation between his condition and sin in this case. Notice Jesus didn't say, "You've got it all wrong. Suffering is just a random event that has nothing to do with sin." Jesus only addressed the specifics of this particular case, in which there was no correlation.

In a broad sense, sickness, disabilities, and even death are all the result of sin. We must remember that Adam and Eve were not created evil, but perfect, immune to aging, never to die. They did have the ability to choose right or wrong, and they made that choice. Had Adam and Eve never sinned, the curse of sin would not have come as a result: "Therefore, just as sin entered the world through one man, and death through sin, and in this way death came to all men, because all sinned" (Rom. 5:12 NIV). The point we must keep in mind is that people—not God—are responsible for sin.

No one will be in hell accidentally.

So why didn't God make man so he couldn't sin? Because He has given us a free will to choose good or evil, to do right or wrong. It seems it would be a much better (and certainly safer) world if God did not allow us to exercise our free will. Free will is our greatest blessing, and in many ways, it is our greatest curse.

But if God did not give us free will, we would be like mere preprogrammed robots. God wants to be loved and obeyed by creatures who voluntarily choose to do so.

After 9/11, the one question I was asked the most was, "Why did God allow this?" Some even asserted that it was God's judgment on the United States. I don't agree. In Luke 13, we find a story that Jesus told about a tower that fell on a group of Gentiles. He asked the rhetorical question, "Do you think they were more guilty than all the others living in Jerusalem? I tell you, no! But unless you repent, you too will all perish" (vv. 4–5). The issue Jesus was addressing was whether this happened to these people because they were horrible sinners. He was essentially saying, "No. People die. Period. But you are a sinner as well. It could happen to you. They were not any worse than you. It happened, and it could happen to you too."

Everyone will eventually die. No one is exempt. This doesn't mean that God is unfair. It doesn't mean that the reason for their dying was God's judgment. It simply means that their time to leave this earth came. And it will come to everyone. The Bible says, "And as it is appointed for men to die once, but after this the judgment" (Heb. 9:27). Some die young. Some die old. Some die slowly. Some die quickly. But everyone dies. We just don't want to deal with that fact.

But if you are a Christian, then you have hope. You know that when you die, you will go into the presence of the Lord. Even so, God, in His mercy, can take the tragedies of life and use them. In fact, there are three ways suffering can work in our lives. It can be corrective, constructive, or allowed to bring glory to God.

Corrective suffering is the idea that God will send some type of pain in our lives to get our attention. Though it was not the case in the story of the blind man in John 9, sometimes sickness *can* come as direct result of our sin. When Jesus healed a paralytic man at the pool of Bethesda, He said, "See, you are well again. Stop sinning or something worse may happen to you" (John 5:14 NIV). So we see that sickness can be the product of our sin. But that very sickness can bring us to Jesus, just as it did with this man. Many people come to Christ because of unexpected sickness, tragedy, the death of a loved one, or through a personal crisis like divorce or addiction to alcohol or drugs.

God can also use sickness or tragedy to correct wayward children. David said, "Your rod and Your staff, they comfort me" (Ps. 23:4). It is a great comfort for me to know that God loves me enough to correct me. It proves that I am His very child. I really can't correct someone else's child, but I can—and should—correct mine. When someone who is deliberately going astray with drinking and partying and gets charged with a DUI, when someone who is lying gets found out, when someone who is rebelling against God becomes ill or is terminated from his or her job, God may be using those circumstances as a means of correction. That is what happened to Jonah. God sent a storm to get his attention. The psalmist wrote, "Before I was afflicted I went astray, but now I keep Your word" (Ps. 119:67).

Humanity has turned against what little it knows to be true.

So when sickness, suffering, tragedy, or hardship comes into our lives, we should say, "Lord, are you trying to tell me something? Because if You are, I'm all ears!" Having gotten your attention, God may then remove that suffering. Or there may be another reason for it.

Constructive suffering would be a time when God is trying to do something in your life to produce a desired result. Paul wrote,

> For our present troubles are small and won't last very long. Yet they produce for us a glory that vastly outweighs them and will last forever! So we don't look at the troubles we can see now; rather, we fix our gaze on things that cannot be seen. For the things we see now will soon be gone, but the things we cannot see will last forever. (2 Cor. 4:17–18 NLT)

When Paul spoke of a physical affliction, a "thorn in the flesh," it was constructive suffering: "To keep me from becoming conceited because of these surpassingly great revelations, there was given me a thorn in my flesh, a messenger of Satan, to torment me" (2 Cor. 12:7 NIV).

Suffering that is allowed in order to glorify God can be the endurance of that suffering, as in Paul's case, or in the life of someone like Joni Eareckson Tada, Corrie ten Boom, or Lt. Col. Brian Birdwell. Joni Eareckson Tada is a quadriplegic from a diving accident from her youth, Corrie ten Boom survived a Nazi concentration camp that took the lives of her father and sister, and Lt. Col. Brian Birdwell was in the Pentagon when the plane hit on 9/11, losing many friends and suffering severe burns over 60 percent of his body. Yet all three have gloried God with their lives, using their difficulties to encourage others to turn to God.

But there are also times when God will glorify himself by removing the suffering. Such was the case with the blind man we read about in John 9: " 'Neither this man nor his parents sinned,' said Jesus, 'but this happened so that the work of God might be displayed in his life. As long as it is day, we must do the work of him who sent me. Night is coming, when no one can work' " (vv. 3–4 NLT). Instead of dealing with how this man ended up blind, Jesus glorified himself through it. He healed this man. And God is still healing people today.

We find this promise of healing in Isaiah:

Surely he took up our infirmities and carried our sorrows, yet we considered him stricken by God, smitten by him, and afflicted. But he was pierced for our transgressions, he was crushed for our iniquities; the punishment that brought us peace was upon him, and by his wounds we are healed. (vv. 4–5 NIV)

Commenting on this same verse, Peter wrote: "He himself bore our sins in his body on the tree, so that we might die to sins and live for righteousness; by his wounds you have been healed" (1 Pet. 2:24 NIV). The word "healed" that Peter used is a verb that always speaks of physical healing in the New Testament and always in connection with physical ailments. So it is clear that God can, when it is in His will, heal us.

So why are some of us still sick? One reason is a simple lack of asking. We "do not have because [we] do not ask" (James 4:2).

Jesus chose to do a miracle in the life of the man who had been born blind. And He can do miracles in our lives as well.

3. How can you Christians say that Jesus is the only way to God? Are you saying that if someone doesn't believe in Him, then they are actually going to hell?

The reason I believe that Jesus Christ is the only way to God is because He said it himself: "I am the way, the truth, and the life. No one comes to the Father except through Me" (John 14:6). Because Jesus was both God and man, He was uniquely qualified to bridge the gap. Acts 4:12 says, "Nor is there salvation in any other, for there is no other name under heaven given among men by which we must be saved."

Some argue, "If people are really sincere in what they believe, then they'll get to heaven." This type of fuzzy, illogical thinking is typical of so many today who make the most important decisions of their lives on the basis of feelings and opinion. But let's take this line of reasoning to its logical conclusion. If it is true that a person who is truly sincere in what he or she believes and tries to live a good life will get to heaven, then Adolf Hitler would be in heaven today. He sincerely believed that what he was doing was right. He had a sincere view of racial supremacy and thought it was "right" to exterminate the Jewish people. "But Hitler was evil!" we protest. Even so, if we follow this line of reasoning about being sincere in one's beliefs, then whose definition do we use to define evil? Yours? Mine? The next-door neighbor's? Is it determined by consensus?

> The real reason people don't come to Christ is that they don't want to be born again.

Of course the fact is that Hitler was indeed evil, and any clear-thinking person would see that. It just goes to show how illogical moral relativism really is when carried out to its end result.

According to one poll, 67 percent of Americans do not believe in absolute truth. Yet to say there is no such thing as absolute truth *is*, in itself, an absolute truth. That is why sincerity is never enough. We must have a set of absolutes to live by. We simply can't make up the rules as we go along.

It is not enough to admire and respect Jesus as a great moral teacher. C. S. Lewis said that someone who would say what Jesus said would not be a great moral teacher—he would be either a lunatic or the devil. We can either reject Jesus or worship Him, but, Lewis concluded, "Let us not come with any patronising nonsense about His being a great human teacher. He has not left that open to us. He did not intend to."[9]

We must examine Jesus' unique claims and make a decision.

4. How can a God of love send people to hell?

To be technical, God doesn't send anyone to hell; we in effect send ourselves there. We need to understand that hell was never created for people, but for the devil and his angels. Matthew 25:41 says, "Then He will also say to those on the left hand, 'Depart from Me, you cursed, into the everlasting fire *prepared for the devil and his angels*'" (emphasis mine). God doesn't want anyone to go to hell. He said, "I have no pleasure in the death of the wicked, but that the wicked turn from his way and live" (Ez. 33:11). And we read in 2 Peter 3:9, "The Lord is not slack concerning His promise, as some count slackness, but is longsuffering toward us, not willing that any should perish but that all should come to repentance."

That is why God sent Jesus to die on the cross. If we reject what He did for us, then "how shall we escape if we neglect so great a salvation? ... " (Heb. 2:3). No one will be in hell accidentally. No one will be in heaven accidentally, either. People do not accidentally become Christians. Becoming a Christian is the result of a choice you make. People will be in heaven because of a deliberate choice, and people will be in hell for the same reason.

So if you end up in hell one day, you will have had to practically climb over Jesus to get there. And in the end, you will have no one to blame but yourself. As C. S. Lewis said, the gates of hell are locked from the inside.[10]

5. What about the people who have never heard the gospel? Will God send them to hell?

God will judge us according to the truth we have received. We will not be held accountable for what we do not know.

This, however, does not excuse us from all responsibility. Otherwise, we might say that ignorance is bliss. No matter where we live on God's planet, we humans were born with "eternity in our hearts" (see Eccl. 3:11), a sense that our lives should have meaning and purpose. We were born with a soul and an inner emptiness. But in spite of an internal compass pointing toward God, we have gone our own way. The Bible tells us we "know the truth about God because he has made it obvious to [us]. For ever since the world was created, people have seen the earth and sky. Through everything God made, they can clearly see his invisible qualities—his eternal power and divine nature … " (Rom. 1:19–20 NLT).

Humanity has turned against what little it knows to be true. Some people insist that they have their own standards they live by. But if we were brutally honest with ourselves, we would have to admit that we can't even live up to our own values.

> God does not want to judge us;
> He wants to forgive us.

Others say, "Well, I am a sincere seeker of truth!" If that is the case, then I am confident they will believe in Jesus. If someone is a true seeker of God, then the Lord will reveal himself to such a person. He promises, "And you will seek Me and find Me, when you search for Me with all your heart" (Jer. 29:13).

But the issue of the moment is what will you do with the truth of the gospel? Knowledge brings responsibility, and people will be held accountable before God for what they know.

The Real Reason People Don't Come to Christ

So what's the real reason people don't come to Christ? The real reason is because they love the darkness and don't want to change. That is why, when you pull out a Bible, some people will visibly recoil. They will insist the Bible is full of contradictions. But most people who say this have never even read the Bible.

The real reason people don't come to Christ is that they don't want to be born again. They want to live in darkness. Jesus said, "And this is the condemnation, that the light has come into the world, and men loved darkness rather than light, because their deeds were evil. For everyone practicing evil hates the light and does not come to the light, lest his deeds should be exposed" (John 3:19–20). This leads to the worst sin one can possibly commit: the sin of unbelief. All sin—even sins such as murder, adultery, stealing, or lying—is forgivable ... except this one. Jesus said, "There is no judgment against anyone who believes in him. But anyone who does not believe in him has already been judged for not believing in God's one and only Son" (John 3:18 NLT).

God does not want to judge us; He wants to forgive us. That is why He sent His only Son to come to Earth, to die in our place, and to rise again from the dead.

And that is why He has called us to "go into all the world and preach the gospel to every creature." There are people today who have honest questions. They just need some straight answers. And with God's help and some attention to His Word, you can provide them.

Five Questions Unbelievers Ask

1. "How do you know that the Bible is the Word of God?"

2. "How could a God of love allow suffering?"

3. "How can you Christians say that Jesus is the only way to God?"

4. "How can a God of love send people to hell?"

5. "What about the people who have never heard the gospel?"

8 Making Disciples

I will let you in on a little secret: I've always had a fear of preaching the gospel. But I had to face that fear one day—and the time came sooner than I expected. I was a young Christian and had planned to attend a baptism service that the church I attended was holding down at Newport Beach. But when I arrived, the service was ending rather than beginning. Even so, a few Christians had stayed behind and were holding an informal worship service on the beach. So I walked over to the little group and sat down. No one was really leading the group. Someone would begin singing a worship song, and then everyone else would join in. I hadn't been there that long when I felt a strong urge to share with the group a Scripture passage I had just read that morning.

> We must pray for discernment
> when we are sharing our faith.

"Uh, excuse me," I said as a song was ending. "I read some Scripture this morning that I would like to share." I nervously read through the passage and then talked a little about what God had shown me from those verses.

When I finished speaking, a girl who had just walked up with her friend said, "Excuse me, Pastor. We missed the baptism, and we were wondering if you could still baptize us?"

I quickly explained that I wasn't a pastor and that I didn't know how to baptize anyone. Even so, I was sensing that God wanted me to help them. So pretty soon, we were all making our way down to the water.

Although I had been baptized myself at this very location and had watched the pastors do baptisms, I really had never paid close attention to how it was actually done. So as best as I could remember, I imitated what I had seen as I slowly lowered the girl down into the water and back up again. Relieved to see her still breathing, I then baptized her friend: "I baptize you in the name of the Father, of the Son, and of the Holy Spirit. ... "

It is not enough to admire or respect Jesus Christ.

Before I knew it, a crowd had gathered on the beach to watch. I felt impressed to preach the gospel to them, and I did so to the best of my ability. And when I was finished speaking, I gave an invitation for people to receive Christ. A few responded, and I ended up baptizing them as well!

That day was a turning point for me. I discovered what it was like to be used of God to bring people to Him. And I have never been the same. It was a bit of a sneak preview of things that were to come later in my life.

This is not something that can only happen for a chosen few. God can and will use us to lead others to Christ. I believe that He can use all believers to fulfill the Great Commission, which was given to every follower of Christ. The issue is not so much ability as it is availability. We simply must be willing.

Expect Excuses

As you approach people and begin to share your faith, you will be hit with a barrage of so-called reasons as to why they don't want to come to Christ. In reality, I would suggest that they are most likely excuses. Excuses are nothing more than fancy lies. They speak of a lack of will. It has been said that "an excuse is the skin of a reason stuffed with a lie." It is something we come up with when we don't want to do something. George Washington said, "It is better to come up with no excuse than a bad one."

Jesus told the story of a king who invited his subjects to a great wedding feast for his son. "But they were not concerned and paid no attention [they ignored and made light of the summons, treating it with contempt] and they went away—one to his farm, another to his business" (Matt. 22:5 AMP). In other words, they made excuses for not accepting the king's invitation.

In the same way, a lot of people have a lot of bad excuses as to why they will not give their lives to Jesus Christ. But there is really only one primary reason.

It is not because they struggle with the gospel philosophically or intellectually. (So remember that the next time you are deep into conversation with a skeptic or agnostic.) The issue is not evolution or the legitimacy of the resurrection of Christ. It is not whether the Bible is "full of contradictions." It is not about where Cain's wife came from or about the person who has never heard the gospel. These, for the most part, are all excuses, plain and simple.

There are exceptions, of course. There are legitimate questions some people have that, when answered, they will be satisfied or at least recognize they are not going to have every possible question answered. Still, there are many others who hide behind those questions because they are using them as excuses. These are the people who are already on their second, third, and fourth questions before you have finished answering their first one.

> If we reject His offer, we will have
> no one to blame but ourselves.

This is why we must pray for discernment when we are sharing our faith. Scripture warns, "Do not give what is holy to the dogs; nor cast your pearls before swine, lest they trample them under their feet, and turn and tear you in pieces" (Matt. 7:6). Pigs don't appreciate pearls, just like my dog does not appreciate certain things. It would be a waste to take him to a movie or a concert. He is not interested in those things, and he is especially not interested in my sermons.

He actually attended Harvest Christian Fellowship before he became my family's dog. He had been in training as a guide dog for the blind, so his trainers brought him every Sunday. He would sit patiently and wait during the worship. But as soon as my message ran past thirty minutes, he would start to audibly groan.

If we are truly seeking, then God will make himself known to us.

So when we are sharing with an unbeliever and all we get is mockery, argument, and rejection, we may just want to terminate the conversation. Then again, if we feel that God is leading us to continue, then we should continue.

There were times when Jesus would not even reveal truth to some people. He never spoke a single word to King Herod, who wanted to see a miracle from Him. Why? Because Herod was not a true seeker. John 2:23–24 offers this additional insight as to why Jesus did not engage certain individuals: "Now when He was in Jerusalem at the Passover, during the feast, many believed in His name when they saw the signs which He did. But Jesus did not commit Himself to them, because He knew all men." Think of all those potential converts. But Jesus knew where their hearts were.

God said He will reveal himself to the true seeker (see Jer. 29:13). If people are genuine seekers of the truth, then they will find their way to Jesus Christ. And if people are genuine seekers of the truth, then Jesus Christ will find their way to them.

By the same token, if people are *not* true seekers of the truth, that will become evident by the excuses they make.

Many will insist that teaching Jesus Christ is the only way to God is narrow, insensitive, and intolerant. Amazingly, this issue has become controversial even in the church today. A 1997 *Los Angeles Times* article reported on a two-day seminar to promote a "theology of pluralism" that opposes the teaching that Jesus Christ is the only way to God. Rev. Ronald F. Thiemann, dean of the Divinity School of Harvard University, was quoted as saying, "There might be non-Christian companions with us who also witness to God's truth."

He said that for the sake of the gospel, Christians need to be open to the Spirit's leading.[11] No, for the sake of the gospel, Christians must proclaim it as it has been written in Scripture. The Spirit's leading will always confirm what is written in the Bible. The Bible is the blueprint that we can follow.

Saying that Christ is the only way to the Father is a bedrock issue of the Christian faith. There can be no compromise here. Paul wrote to the believers in Galatia:

> I am astonished that you are so quickly deserting the one who called you by the grace of Christ and are turning to a different gospel—which is really no gospel at all. Evidently some people are throwing you into confusion and are trying to pervert the gospel of Christ. But even if we or an angel from heaven should preach a gospel other than the one we preached to you, let him be eternally condemned! (Gal. 1:6–8 NIV)

The real reason people don't want to hear the gospel is they don't want to change.

It's an either-or proposition. If we declare anything less, then we are preaching a false gospel. People may want to believe that all roads lead to God. They may sincerely hope that every religion is basically true and that they somehow all blend together beautifully. But they don't.

Where Beliefs Collide

For example, concerning the existence of a personal God, Buddhists deny it altogether. Hindus believe that God is formless and abstract, taking the form of a trinity as well as the form of millions of lesser gods. In direct contrast, the Bible teaches that God is a personal deity who created us in His own image, loves us, and wants to have a relationship with us.

Concerning salvation, Buddhists believe salvation comes by self-effort alone, with no personal God to help or guide you. Hindus believe salvation is achieved by devotion, works, and self-control.

Muslims insist that man pays for his own sins, earns his own salvation, and can never be certain whether salvation has been achieved. In contrast, the Bible teaches that Jesus Christ died for our sins. Salvation is a free gift of God, apart from works, given to us by a personal God. It also teaches that we can have the absolute assurance of heaven when we die.

You can play a key role in a new believer's life.

Concerning Jesus Christ, Buddhists believe that Jesus was a good teacher, but less important than Buddha. Hindus believe that Jesus was just one of many incarnations, or sons of God. They teach that Christ was not the one and only Son of God, that He was no more divine than any other man, and that He did not die for our sins. Muslims will tell you that Jesus Christ was only a man—a prophet equal to Adam, Noah, or Abraham, all of whom are below Mohammed in importance. The Koran teaches that Christ did not die for the sins of humanity, but that Judas, not Jesus, died on the cross. They believe that Judas was mistaken for Jesus, and that Christ lived a long life. Muslims also reject the preexistence of Jesus and His death and resurrection.

In direct contrast, the Bible teaches that Jesus Christ was God in human form. He was the one and only Son of God. He was and is the Savior of the world who died and rose again and who will personally come into the heart of and transform the one who calls on Him.

So you see, it doesn't work to believe in all of the above. The tenets of these extremely diverse religions directly contradict one another. They simply cannot all be true. Buddhists, Muslims, and Hindus have no assurance they will get to heaven. Only Christianity holds to that wonderful, life-transforming hope.

We've Been Warned

As I wrote earlier, it is not enough to admire or respect Jesus Christ or to merely think of Him as a great moral teacher. We must examine His unique claims and make a decision.

Imagine driving up a freeway off-ramp marked, "DANGER! DO NOT ENTER!" Police are frantically waving you back, but still you persist in driving the wrong way. If you die, who would be at fault? It wouldn't be the highway department or law enforcement. It wouldn't be the company that manufactured your car. It would be you.

That is why God sent His only Son, Jesus, who is saying to all of humanity, "Stop! Turn around! Why will you die in your sins? Put your faith in Me and find forgiveness and everlasting life."

If we reject His offer, we will have no one to blame but ourselves. On the other hand, if we are truly seeking, then God will make himself known to us.

The Bible mentions a Roman centurion named Cornelius who was a very religious man. He prayed and sought God, although he knew very little, if anything, about Jesus Christ. God answered his prayers and sent Peter to preach the gospel to him. When Cornelius heard that wonderful message, he believed. Not only that, but everyone in his household became believers as well. That is because Cornelius was a true seeker.

> ## For many new believers, the problem is acclimating to the Christian life.

Quite often, the people who ask challenging questions and attempt to sidetrack you as you're sharing the gospel are throwing up a smokescreen to keep you at bay. They really don't want to know whether Jesus is the only way to God, nor are they concerned about some Stone Age tribe that has never heard the gospel. In reality, such a person simply doesn't want to hear about personal responsibility before a holy God and feels compelled to lock your mental gears with questions.

The real reason people don't want to hear the gospel is they don't want to change. That is why we need to pray for them. We need to pray that they will turn from the darkness to light and from the power of Satan to the power of God.

Pop the Question!

So, having answered the questions that have been asked of you, what do you do next? Now is the time to close the deal, so to speak. Maybe the reason that many of us have never led another person to Christ is because we have never officially "popped the question."

God has not given us the privilege of hearing His Word so we can become sermon connoisseurs.

I never officially did that with my wife Cathe. Rather than getting down on one knee and proposing to her, I said, "Well, I guess we're going to get married!" Cathe wasn't even sure that I had proposed until later. Somehow we decided to get married, but Cathe doesn't ever remember a formal, official proposal on my part, and neither do I.

So it is important for us to ask, "Would you like to ask Jesus Christ into your life right now?" It isn't necessary to push or pressure someone, but we should simply and prayerfully ask.

The No Answer

The answer might be, "I don't feel ready yet." That is a good time to ask why, and if you can help in any way. The answer still might be no, but you can explain how they could pray later, if they choose, adding, "I am confident that God will respond, because He said, 'You will seek Me and find Me, when you search for Me with all your heart.'"

The Yes Answer

The answer also might be yes. So go ahead and pray with him or her at that moment. What a joy it is to pray with someone to make this commitment, or to bring a person to church or a crusade and see him or her walk forward at the invitation! The Bible says there is joy in heaven over one sinner who comes to repentance (see Luke 15:7).

Start Discipling

So once you've prayed with someone to make a commitment to Christ, is that the end of it? No. That is the beginning. Now it is your privilege—and your responsibility—to disciple this person. Going back to the Great Commission, we are commanded to "Go therefore and *make disciples of all the nations,* baptizing them in the name of the Father and of the Son and of the Holy Spirit, *teaching them* to observe all things that I have commanded you … " (Matt. 28:19–20, emphasis mine). We often emphasize the "go" of this verse, only to overlook the aspect of making disciples and teaching them. It means reproducing ourselves.

We are first to be disciples of Jesus Christ and then we are to repeat the process: "So we tell others about Christ, warning everyone and teaching everyone with all the wisdom God has given us. We want to present them to God, perfect in their relationship to Christ" (Col. 1:28 NLT). Paul wrote to Timothy, "You have heard me teach things that have been confirmed by many reliable witnesses. Now teach these truths to other trustworthy people who will be able to pass them on to others" (2 Tim. 2:2 NLT).

> ## You need the outlet as much as they need the input.

I am so thankful someone did this for me. After I accepted Christ during that lunch hour on my high school campus, no one gave me a Bible that day or prayed with me afterward. I was on my own. So the next weekend, I went off to the woods to do drugs. But God spoke to my heart that weekend and told me, "You don't need that anymore."

The following Monday, a Christian named Mark walked up to me at school and said, "Hi, I saw you at the Bible study, and I noticed you went forward and accepted Christ."

"Yeah," I responded defensively.

"Well," he said. "I am a Christian, and I want to help you get strong spiritually. Do you have a Bible?"

"No, I don't have one yet."

Mark gave me a Bible and invited me to go to worship services with him. He drove me to church, where he introduced me to other Christians. He invited me over to his house, where I met his parents, who were also Christians. Mark and his family patiently answered my questions and showed me what it was like to be a Christian in the real world, and I desperately needed that. I was able to actually *see* how to live the Christian life.

God wants to use you to fulfill the Great Commission.

The Book of Acts tells the story of Apollos, a powerful preacher in the early church. He didn't quite have his doctrine straight, but he had plenty of passion. So a Christian couple, Aquila and Priscilla, took him under their wing. The Bible says that "when Aquila and Priscilla heard him, they took him aside and explained to him the way of God more accurately" (Acts 18:26). That is called discipling.

We are not all called to be preachers like Apollos or Paul. Some of us are called to work behind the scenes in this crucial role of discipleship. We tend to hear a lot about Paul, but we don't hear all that much about two men who played a key role in his life: Ananias and Barnabas. They didn't write any books of the New Testament, and there are no biblical accounts of their performing miracles by the hand of God. They never preached any sermons that we know of. But they did influence a man who touched millions and millions. Ananias and Barnabas were heroes of the church.

You may not consider yourself a biblical scholar, but you can play a key role in a new believer's life. For many new believers, the problem is acclimating to the Christian life. They need teaching, but they also need a personal example. In short, they need a friend.

Later in his life, Paul carried on the ministry of discipling with young Timothy: "But you, Timothy, certainly know what I teach, and how I live, and what my purpose in life is. You know my faith, my patience, my love, and my endurance" (2 Tim. 2:10 NLT). That kind of personal knowledge comes from spending time with someone.

And Paul wrote to the church at Thessalonica, "As you know how we exhorted, and comforted, and charged every one of you, as a father does his own children, that you would walk worthy of God who calls you into His own kingdom and glory" (1 Thess. 2:11–12).

Not only does discipleship benefit new believers, but it also benefits us. You see, after we have been Christians for a time, we need an outlet for what we are learning. God has not given us the privilege of hearing His Word so we can become sermon connoisseurs. We are to take what He has given and share it with others. I am firmly convinced that to maintain input without output is hazardous to our spiritual growth and progress. We as believers can be in serious danger if, in our attendance of Bible studies, prayer meetings, and intake of spiritual information, we do not have an adequate outlet for our newfound truths. In our evangelizing and discipling of others, we not only save sinners from hell, but we also save ourselves from spiritual stagnation.

If you were to take a new believer under your wing, it could bring revival to your life. Whether it's leading a person to Christ or discipling someone who has just accepted Him, you need the outlet as much as they need the input.

New believers need our wisdom, knowledge, and experience as more mature believers. And we as mature believers need their childlike simplicity of faith, their zeal, and their first-love relationship with Jesus.

It's like going to Disneyland with adults versus going there with children. When you go with adults, what do you want to do first (after complaining about how expensive it is)? You want to eat. But after you eat, you're not ready to go on any rides—you're ready to take a nap. You get in line anyway and then complain about how long the wait is.

But when you go to Disneyland with children, it is a different experience altogether. It is all so real to them. I remember when I first took my sons there. I loved pointing out Sleeping Beauty's Castle and watching their expressions when they spotted Mickey Mouse walking down the street. When you look at it through the eyes of a child, it becomes a whole new experience.

That is why I'm so excited to have a granddaughter now. My sons don't get excited about Disneyland anymore, but I know that she will.

When you take a new believer under your wing and see life the way a new believer sees it, it will bring back things you have forgotten. It will rekindle your fire. That is why you need to do everything you can to try to bring people to Christ, and at the very least, find someone who is new in the faith and offer to help them grow spiritually. The Bible says, "The generous soul will be made rich, and he who waters will also be watered himself" (Prov. 11:25).

Maybe God will never call you to be a pastor or a missionary. But what if you answered God's call to disciple someone He has brought into your life and that person went on to change the world? You would have the joy of knowing that you played an important role in his or her life. As Daniel 12:3 says, "Those who are wise shall shine like the brightness of the firmament, and those who turn many to righteousness like the stars forever and ever."

God wants to use you to fulfill the Great Commission. Let's pray that the Lord will use us in these critical and strategic times in which we are living. Because the harvest is great, but the laborers are few.

Where Christianity Conflicts (with Other World Religions)

- The existence of a personal God: God loves us and wants to have a relationship with us.

- Salvation apart from works: Salvation is a free gift of God, apart from works, given to us by a personal God.

- The deity of Jesus Christ: Jesus Christ was God in human form. He was the one and only Son of God. He was and is the Savior of the world who died and rose again.

Afterword

This book has been devoted to the subject of taking the gospel to people who don't know the Lord. Maybe you are one of them. Jesus Christ is a personal God who can be known and who can forgive you of all of your sins and come and live inside of you. Did you know that? And have you responded?

If you were to die today, do you know for certain whether you would go to heaven? Or, are you afraid you would be one of those who would go to hell?

Jesus Christ, who died on the cross and rose again from the dead, stands at the door of your life and knocks. He says, "I stand at the door and knock. If you hear my voice and open the door, I will come in" (Rev. 3:20 NLT).

Have you asked Him to come into your life? If not, you can do that today. When I came to Christ on my high school campus, I was one of the last people to go forward. Jesus said, "Come to me, all you who are weary and burdened, and I will give you rest" (Matt. 11:28 NIV). You can come to Jesus with your questions. You can come to Him with your problems. You can come to Him with your sins and even with your addictions. You will not regret this decision. Here is what you need to do:

1. *Realize that you are a sinner.* No matter how good of a life we try to live, we still fall miserably short of being a good person. That is because we are all sinners. We all fall short of God's desire for us to be holy. The Bible says, "No one is good—not even one" (Romans 3:10 NLT). This is because we cannot become who we are supposed to be without Jesus Christ.

2. *Recognize that Jesus Christ died on the cross for you.* The Bible tells us, "But God showed His great love for us by sending Christ to die for us while were still sinners" (Romans 5:8 NLT). This is the Good News, that God loves us so much that, when we least deserved it, He sent His only Son to die in our place.

3. *Repent of your sin.* The Bible tells us to "repent and be converted" (Acts 3:19). The word "repent" means "to change our direction in life." Instead of running away from God, we can run toward Him.

4. *Receive Jesus Christ into your life.* Becoming a Christian is not merely believing some creed or going to church on Sunday. It is having Christ himself take residence in your life and heart.

If you would like to invite Jesus Christ into your life, simply pray a prayer like this one, and mean it in your heart:

Dear Lord Jesus, I know I am a sinner. I believe You died for my sins. Right now, I turn from my sins and open the door of my heart and life. I confess You as my personal Lord and Savior. Thank You for saving me. Amen.

The Bible tells us, "If we confess our sins, he is faithful and just to forgive us our sins and cleanse us from all unrighteousness" (1 John 1:9). If you just prayed that prayer and meant it, then Jesus Christ has now taken residence in your heart. Your decision to follow Christ means that God has forgiven your sins. You have the assurance that you will go to heaven when you die, and you will find that meaning and purpose in life that you have been searching for all this time.

To help you grow in your newfound faith, be sure to make the following a part of your life each day: read the Bible regularly, pray, spend time with other Christians by going to church, and tell others about your faith in Christ.

For additional resources to help you learn more about what it means to be a follower of Jesus Christ, please visit http://www.harvest.org/knowgod/.

Notes

1. Billy Graham, *Just As I Am: The Autobiography of Billy Graham* (San Francisco: HarperCollins Publishers, 1999), 565.

2. C. H. Spurgeon, *Metropolitan Tabernacle Pulpit,* vol. 22, (Pasadena, Tex.: Pilgrim Publications, 1971), 143–144.

3. Allen G. Breed and Binaj Gurubacharya, "Everest Remains Deadly Draw for Climbers," *USATODAY.com,* July 16, 2006, http://www.usatoday.com/tech/science/2006-07-16-everest-david-sharp_x.htm.

4. C. S. Lewis, *Mere Christianity: A Revised and Amplified Edition, with a New Introduction* (San Francisco: HarperCollins Publishers, 2001), 155.

5. Adapted from *How to Share Your One-Minute Message* (Riverside, Calif.: Harvest Ministries, 2003).

6. Dr. Carl Wieland, "Hopeful Monsters Revisited," *Answersin Genesis.org,* http://www.answersingenesis.org/creation/v1/i1/hopeful.asp.

7. C. S. Lewis, *The Weight of Glory* (San Francisco: Harper Collins Publishers, 2001), 140.

8. Dr. Nelson Glueck, *Rivers in the Desert: A History of the Negev* (Philadelphia: Jewish Publication Society of America, 1959), 31.

9. C. S. Lewis, *Mere Christianity,* 52.

10. C. S. Lewis, *Made for Heaven: And Why on Earth It Matters* (San Francisco: HarperCollins Publishers, 2005), ix.

11. Larry B. Stammer, "No Religion Has a Monopoly on God's Truth, Clerics Assert," *The Los Angeles Times* (February 1, 1997), 4.

About the Author

Greg Laurie is the pastor of Harvest Christian Fellowship in Riverside, California, one of the fifteen largest churches in the United States. He is the author of more than thirty books, including the Gold Medallion Award winner, *The Upside-Down Church,* as well as *Losers and Winners, Saints and Sinners* and *The Best Is Yet to Come.* You can find his study notes in the *New Believer's Bible* and the *Seeker's Bible.* Host of the *Knowing God with Greg Laurie* television program and the nationally syndicated radio program, *A New Beginning,* Greg Laurie is also the founder and featured speaker for Harvest Crusades—contemporary, large-scale evangelistic outreaches, which local churches organize nationally and internationally. He has also appeared on CNN's *Larry King Live, ABC World News Tonight, Fox News,* and *MSNBC,* sharing how the Bible is relevant for people today. Greg Laurie holds two honorary doctorates from Biola University and Azusa Pacific University and serves on the board of directors of the Billy Graham Evangelistic Association and Samaritan's Purse. He and his wife Cathe live in Southern California and have two children and one grandchild.

Other Allen David Books
Published by
Kerygma Publishing

The Great Compromise

For Every Season: Daily Devotions

Strengthening Your Marriage

Marriage Connections

Are We Living in the Last Days?

"I'm Going on a Diet Tomorrow"

Strengthening Your Faith

Deepening Your Faith

Living Out Your Faith

Dealing with Giants

Secrets to Spiritual Success

How to Know God

*10 Things You Should Know
About God and Life*

For Every Season, vol. 2

*The Greatest Story Ever Told:
Volume One: Great Encounters with God*

Visit: www.kerygmapublishing.com
www.allendavidbooks.com
www.harvest.org